GOD'S PROPHETIC CALENDAR

GOD'S PROPHETIC CALENDAR

Lehman Strauss

LOIZEAUX BROTHERS
Neptune, New Jersey

First Edition, December 1987

Printed in the United States of America.

A publication of Loizeaux Brothers, Inc.
A nonprofit organization devoted to the Lord's work and to the spread of His truth.

All Scripture quotations are from the *Authorized King James Version*.

Library of Congress Cataloging-in-Publication Data

Strauss, Lehman.
    God's prophetic calendar.

    Bibliography: p.
    1. Fasts and feasts in the Bible—Typology.
2. Bible.   O.T.   Leviticus XXIII—Criticism, interpretation, etc.   I. Title.
BS1199.F35S77   1987   222'.13064   87-16891
ISBN 0-87213-816-X

Contents

CONTENTS

God's Calendar

EVERY YEAR NEAR LABOR DAY I can count on the beginning of an influx of calendars. Almost daily for the next four months my mailbox will have at least one calendar in it. They come from Bible institutes, colleges, seminaries, mission boards, radio and television preachers, insurance agents, morticians. Now, I do not need a hundred or more calendars every year, but I do need at least one. I could not carry on my ministry without one. For most of us the calendar is indispensable.

The idea of the calendar originated with God, but it was for man's benefit. God does not need a calendar. He is not a victim of time. "But, beloved, be not ignorant of this one thing, that one day is with the Lord as a thousand years, and a thousand years as one day" (2 Peter 3:8). God did not prepare a calendar to keep Himself informed of His future plans, but He did arrange one for the human race, presenting it first to the young nation of Israel.

The calendar we are about to examine shows God's plan for the human race beginning with the death of the Lord Jesus Christ at Calvary, followed by His bodily resurrection from death and the grave, His ascension to heaven, the beginning of the church at Pentecost, the present church age, the appearing of our Lord to translate the church to heaven, the tribulation that follows the church's rapture, the regathering and regeneration of Israel, and the return of Messiah to reign on earth.

God's prophetic calendar containing all of the above events

7

is recorded in one chapter in the Bible. All of these future events are to be located in various parts of the Bible, but in Leviticus 23 they all are presented in sequence. I have not located a single chapter in the Bible that, in my judgment, is more doctrinally and prophetically profound and fraught with more of the weight of God's plan for holy living, than the twenty-third chapter of Leviticus. Here is an orderly unfolding of the prophetic panorama, reserved in clarity for the student who will take the time to study it carefully. Here the student will see the prophetic and practical import unfold in progressive and harmonious array.

Before commencing our study of this chapter in Leviticus, it will prove helpful if we take note of some features about the book itself. While it is true that each book in the Bible is an entity in itself and that each contains its own peculiar message, no one book can be disassociated from the remaining sixty-five. Leviticus follows logically and progressively after Exodus as Exodus follows Genesis.

> In Genesis man is ruined by sin.
> In Exodus man is redeemed by sacrifice.
> In Leviticus man is regulated for service.
> In Exodus the tabernacle is erected for the purpose of worshiping God.
> In Leviticus the tabernacle is entered for the practice of worshiping God.

In Exodus Israel was redeemed from the bondage of Egypt, after which God gave instructions to Moses for the building of the tabernacle. The tabernacle was decreed and designed by God Himself to be occupied by Him. He had said, "And let them make me a sanctuary, that I may dwell among them"

8

(Exodus 25:8). It was God's plan to be in the midst of His redeemed people so that they might worship and serve Him.

Now how will these redeemed people go about the business of worshiping and serving the one true and living God? They could organize a committee, or even elect one person from among them to draw up ways and means for worship. There would be the need for ministers and a variety of services. How should the people approach God? What would be the necessary requirements for worship? What should be the best time for gathering the people to worship? These questions, and many more, would need answers.

But even redeemed people are incapable of knowing how to worship the one true and holy God. One distinguishing characteristic of worship is that God Himself is preeminently present among His people. The whole of the believer's life must be lived out in the presence of God. And so Leviticus is a book of laws given by God to regulate the worship of His people. Every offering was to be presented "unto the LORD" (Leviticus 1:2,9,13-14,17; 2:2,8-9,12,14,16; 3:5-6,9,11,14, etc.) and offered "before the LORD" (1:3,5,11). The thoughts, words, and deeds of the worshiper were to be offered unto the Lord and before His presence.

Only God Himself could write the rules and regulations for worship because He is the only one who must be satisfied. Leviticus is, by its own testimony, the Word of God given to Moses for the children of Israel (1:1-2; 4:1-2; 5:14; 6:1,8,19,24; 7:22,28,35-38; 8:1). After all, the holy God was the offended person. Man was the sinner who caused the offence. The sinner could not qualify to prescribe rules for worship.

In Leviticus 9 we have a clear picture of how sinners must worship a holy God. The erection of the tabernacle had been completed; the solemn ceremony of ordaining the priests had come to its close; God had given instructions as to how the solemn service of worship was to be conducted in the tabernacle. All was going according to the divine plan when suddenly a tragedy struck. Chapter 10 records that incident which interrupted the worship of the Lord: "And Nadab and Abihu, the sons of Aaron, took either of them his censer, and put fire therein, and put incense thereon and offered strange fire before the LORD, which he commanded them not. And there went out fire from the LORD, and devoured them, and they died before the LORD" (Leviticus 10:1-2).

Aaron had four sons: Nadab, Abihu, Eleazar, and Ithamar. The older two, Nadab and Abihu, accompanied their father and Moses, along with seventy of the elders of Israel, to a special service of worship (Exodus 24:1). Apparently, this was a part of their training for the office of priest, to which office they were subsequently ordained (Leviticus 8:30).

The precise sin of which Nadab and Abihu were guilty is not stated clearly in the Bible, so that we cannot be dogmatic in an attempt to identify it. Some suppose that they used ingredients in the preparation of the incense that were not divinely approved (see Exodus 30:9,34-38), or that they used fire other than the "burning coals of fire from off the altar" (Leviticus 16:12), or that they offered the incense at a time not designated in the order of worship. Whatever the exact nature of their sin, we know it was a violation of a definite command given by God.

We cannot judge their motive nor question their sincerity, but we do know that according to God's law they committed a sin worthy of death. God's rules for worshiping Him must be obeyed promptly and perfectly. Why? Because God demands that in all worship He must be sanctified in them that come near to Him, and glorified before all the people (Leviticus 10:3). John Calvin wrote: "If we reflect how holy a thing God's

10

worship is, the enormity of the punishment will by no means offend us." No one will deny that much of what passes for worship today is "strange fire."

At this point in the narrative God spoke a personal word to Aaron: "Do not drink wine nor strong drink, thou, nor thy sons with thee, when ye go into the tabernacle of the congregation, lest ye die: it shall be a statute for ever throughout your generations" (Leviticus 10:9). It is possible that the behavior of Nadab and Abihu resulted from their being under the influence of alcoholic beverage. Alcohol has a way of confusing and controlling the mind, a condition that renders one incapable of worshiping God.

Now read verses 9 and 10 with verse 8 because the three verses comprise one complete sentence: "And that ye may put difference between holy and unholy, and between unclean and clean. And that ye may teach the children of Israel all the statutes which the LORD hath spoken unto them by the hand of Moses" (Leviticus 10:10-11). One can see the connection between the command in verse 9 and the reason for the command in verse 10. The use of alcohol is obviously related to the "unholy" and "unclean." Under the influence of alcohol one cannot distinguish clearly between holy and unholy as was seen in the behavior of Nadab and Abihu.

One reading of the book of Leviticus will show that its major theme is holiness. God is holy. He demands holiness and has made every provision for it. The word "holy" appears not less than ninety-one times. Repeatedly, God says to His people, "Ye shall be holy; for I am holy" (Leviticus 11:44-45; 19:1; 20:7,26; 21:8). Unholy is the converse of holy. Anything that is not holy is unholy. Even God's name, which expresses His character, is holy (20:3; 22:2,32). The Bible requires holiness in the life of all who would worship a holy God.

11

The many denominations and branches of Christendom have their multiple variations of worship with each defending its own approach as the correct one. This subject was brought up in a women's Bible study group to which I was invited to speak. After a general free-for-all discussion, most of the women present were satisfied with the idea that there are many ways to worship God. One woman said, "You worship God in your way, and I'll worship Him my way, and my way satisfies me." It was obvious that she had no idea of the biblical concept of worship. The big question is not, Am I satisfied with my motive and manner of worship? but rather, Is God satisfied? I fear that much which passes for worship today is "strange fire." The message of the book of Leviticus leaves no doubt as to the requirements and regulations for the worship of the one true God. Man needs divine guidance in this business of worship; therefore, God arranged a calendar to guide him.

Leviticus 23 is that calendar. While the calendar was given originally to the nation Israel, the events listed in it reach forward to the present church age and even beyond.

When we study a given passage of Scripture, we should look for three things:

1. *The primary association of the passage.* To whom was it spoken? Why did God speak thus? We know that Leviticus 23 was given originally to the Jewish people. In its primary association, these rules and regulations were drawn up by God Himself and intended for the nation Israel. "And the LORD spake unto Moses, saying, Speak unto the children of Israel . . ." (Leviticus 23:1-2).

2. *The prophetic anticipation in the passage.* Does it contain a prediction of the future? Does its message have an immediate and a future fulfillment? Does this ancient chapter in the Bible tell us only what God has done, or does it include what He is

doing now and what He is going to do in the future?

3. *The personal application in the passage.* Is there a message for the Christian today in the book of Leviticus? The New Testament teaches that "all Scripture is given by inspiration of God, and is profitable . . ." (2 Timothy 3:16). Can we assume, therefore, that basic principles of behavior as recorded in the Old Testament are applicable in the lives of Christians today? Have God's basic rules for worship changed? Leviticus sets forth some God-given absolutes for a godly lifestyle. These moral, social, and ethical basics never change. They stand for all of time and are apropos to us today.

In speaking of the two Testaments, someone has said that the New is in the Old concealed, and the Old is in the New revealed. Typology is the nexus that brings the two Testaments together in proper perspective. Within this one chapter is a series of types serving to give an outline of God's dealings with His earthly people Israel.

Here too is to be seen the longest range of God's program of salvation to be found in any single chapter in the Old Testament. It stretches from Calvary to eternity future.

God made an unconditional covenant with Abraham. This covenant, which must of necessity stand forever, He later confirmed to Isaac and to Jacob. When He brought the children of Israel out of Egypt, He taught them in types in order that His plan for them might jut out in bold outline far beyond the immediate generations to whom Moses wrote. Leviticus 23 projects more prophecy and presents more of God's plan for Israel than any other chapter we can call to mind. Step by step, from commencement to consummation, the divine purpose graphically unfolds.

The seven feasts instituted in this chapter God claims as "the feasts of the LORD . . . my feasts" (verse 2). The Revised Version aptly terms them as "appointed seasons." They were holy holidays. Having been appointed by Jehovah, they were ceremoniously set apart by Him to keep the people in close-linked fellowship with Him as well as to encourage affectionate, willing service to Him. Jehovah was the host, His people were His guests. To have His own, whom He redeemed, come together and rejoice in Him was the delight of His loving heart. It staggers one's mind to ponder the thought that we worthless creatures afford the great God of eternity His complete delight. John Ritchie has well said, "How poor and miserable are the subjects that occasion mirth and gladness among the sons of men compared with these! And how soon they fade away, and are forgotten! But Heaven's enjoyments last; they do not lose their charm."

Although these were not the only feasts that comprised Israel's sacred calendar and this is not the only passage where these particular ones are mentioned, they are unique in a twofold sense. First, they voice a special communication from Jehovah to Moses, and second, they are brought together in an orderly and comprehensive way. Each separate feast had a distinctive import all its own, yet when the seven are arranged in their chronological order, we can see how they were divinely preordained to typify future events.

An expressive word to observe is *convocation*. It appears no less than ten times in this chapter (Leviticus 23:2,3,4,7,8,21, 27,35,36,37). The word means "a calling together" or "an assembly." The feasts were regular annual get-togethers. Actually, the seven holy holidays brought the people together to Jerusalem three times each year, all seven being held during the three assemblings. These conferences brought Jewish believers together who otherwise would not be able to fellowship with one another at any other time. What happy occasions

14

and what times of refreshment! It was the season to encourage and comfort one another.

Even today it delights the heart of God to have His people come together to express their joy in Him and His Word. One important fact to be noted is that the gatherings are called "holy convocations." They were set apart by God for spiritual emphases. One of the main lessons taught in the book of Leviticus is holiness.

Our fellowship is with the Father (1 John 1:3) and with His Son (1 Corinthians 1:9) and with the Holy Spirit (Philippians 2:1) and with one another (1 John 1:7). We have fellowship with God only in Jesus Christ and through the Holy Spirit. Sweet fellowship with Him is fundamental to pleasant fellowship with one another. More than fundamental, it is the only ground for fellowship with others of like faith. Christian fellowship is not the fellowship of one denomination, assembly, sect, or one group with another of that same denomination, assembly, sect, or group, but of any or all true believers in the Lord Jesus Christ. It is not mere companionship, but a communion of thought, interest, and affection.

Cogently, the New Testament sets forth the degeneration of these feasts from the holy, solemn occasions God intended them to be, to the cold, formal, religious festivals of hypocrisy that man made them to become. Particularly during the lifetime of our Lord Jesus Christ this was true. While crowds journeyed from diverse parts of Palestine to Jerusalem to keep the feasts, the references are not to "the feasts of the Lord" but to "the Jews' passover" (John 2:13), "a feast of the Jews" (John 5:1), and "the Jews' feast of tabernacles" (John 7:2). Even long before Christ came, Jehovah had said, "Your new moons and your appointed feasts my soul hateth: they are a trouble to me; I am weary to bear them" (Isaiah 1:14). They were no longer "the feasts of the LORD." As God saw the behavior of His people He could not call them "my feasts." What began as holy convocations had now become unholy convocations.

Here, we may learn how possible it is for holy things to lose their energizing power and vernal freshness. How easy it is for Christians to heartlessly participate in worship through careless, formal, and irreverent forms. Let us search our hearts at all times so that we might not slip into a void form of worship that would weary our loving Lord. In our Lord's day the Jews held the feasts but the Lord was absent.

A special reference is made to men attending the set feasts. "Three times in a year shall all thy males appear before the LORD thy God in the place which he shall choose, in the feast of unleavened bread, and in the feast of weeks, and in the feast of tabernacles: and they shall not appear before the LORD empty" (Deuteronomy 16:16). It might appear that in those days, as now, some men were negligent in attending to spiritual matters. The man is to be the head of the house, holding rightful authority from God. If the man gives due attention to the appointed times for worship, he has a better chance of leading his family to respond to the will of God. (This special announcement to the men is recorded also in Exodus 23:17; 34:23.)

I believe that God wants His children to pay attention to this important fact. Men were so essential in the work of the Lord that no matter where a man was or what he was doing, he ceased from his activity and went to Jerusalem to worship Jehovah at the set feasts. Meeting with God and God's people at appointed times can be one evidence of spiritual health and prosperity. When we are right in our hearts toward God and toward His children, we will rejoice in assembling ourselves together and say with David, "I was glad when they said unto me, Let us go into the house of the LORD" (Psalm 122:1) and with the writer of Hebrews who said, "Not forsaking the assembling of ourselves together" (Hebrews 10:25).

God promised to care for the land and the possessions of His people while they were in Jerusalem keeping His feasts. He said, "Thrice in the year shall all your men children appear before the LORD God, the God of Israel. For I will cast out the nations before thee, and enlarge thy borders: neither shall any man desire thy land, when thou shalt go up to appear before the LORD thy God thrice in the year" (Exodus 34:23-24). The Lord had actually pledged Himself to guard the property of His people if they would serve and worship Him faithfully. "When a man's ways please the LORD, he maketh even his enemies to be at peace with him" (Proverbs 16:7).

Observe further that they were not only to leave their lands and possessions to go to the feasts, but that they were not to appear before the Lord "empty" (Exodus 23:15; Deuteronomy 16:16), that is, they were to bring to Him their sacrificial gifts. If the Israelites were like some of us, they might excuse themselves on the ground that they could not afford to take time off from work to assemble before the Lord. But God sees to it that no man is a loser when he renders willing and cheerful obedience to His commands. After all, we owe our very lives and all we have to Him. "What hast thou that thou didst not receive? Now if thou didst receive it, why dost thou glory, as if thou hadst not received it?" (1 Corinthians 4:7). We who are the Lord's people cannot afford not to obey Him in these holy matters.

God's demands upon His children must be our first concern. When we gladly give Him His due, we always prosper. "But seek ye first the kingdom of God and his righteousness; and all these things shall be added unto you" (Matthew 6:33). His bread and water are most sure to all who walk in the ways of the Lord (Isaiah 33:15-16). Solomon put God first and he prospered abundantly (1 Kings 3:11-13). To make the obtaining of money, food, clothing, and shelter the obsession and goal of life and labor is to tragically miss the ultimate aim in life. Such may be the standard of those who know not the Lord, but it most certainly cannot be the touchstone of the true child of God. The redeemed know that they are heirs of the kingdom, and so they lay all at God's disposal instead of hoarding earthly treasures.

There are seven set feasts, excluding the Sabbath. The number seven is prominent throughout the chapter appearing no fewer than eighteen times. Seven is the number of completion, so we have suggested here a perfect typical outline of God's dealings with the Jew and the Gentile from first to last. The feasts can be divided into two sections of four and three respectively, with an interval between the fourth and fifth feasts. In the seven secrets (or seven mysteries) set forth in our Lord's parables in Matthew 13, the same division exists.

The first four feasts, and the interval between the fourth and fifth, contain truth of God's dealings with mankind up to and including the present dispensation of the church. The last three feasts are intended to teach truths concerning a future dispensation and God's future dealings with Israel. The seven feasts comprise God's calendar.

The following is a list of the feasts in their numerical structure and dispensational setting:

1. The Feast of Passover (Leviticus 23:4-5 cf. Exodus 12:1-14; 1 Corinthians 5:7).
2. The Feast of Unleavened Bread (Leviticus 23:6-8 cf. Exodus 12:15-20: 1 Corinthians 5:6-8).

3. The Feast of Firstfruits (Leviticus 23:9-14 cf. 1 Corinthians 15:20-23).

4. The Feast of Weeks (Leviticus 23:15-21 cf. Acts 2:1).

5. The Feast of Trumpets (Leviticus 23:23-25 cf. 1 Corinthians 15:51-52; 1 Thessalonians 4:16-17; Isaiah 27:12-13).

6. The Feast of Atonement (Leviticus 23:26-32 cf. Leviticus 16).

7. The Feast of Tabernacles (Leviticus 23:33-34 cf. Nehemiah 8:13-17; Zechariah 14:16-19).

PART ONE
The First Coming of Christ

Leviticus 23:1-22

God's Plan of Salvation
God's Provision for Sanctification
God's Pledge of Security
God's Promise of the Spirit

1

The Feast of Passover

God's Plan of Salvation

Leviticus 23:4-5

Since we are assured that the things "written aforetime were written for our learning" (Romans 15:4), and that all Scripture is God-breathed and profitable, we shall find the Old Testament Scriptures rich in types of New Testament truths. One of the richest sections is the book of Leviticus, chapter 23.

J. W. H. NICHOLS

1

The Feast of Passover

God's Plan of Salvation

Leviticus 23:4-5

These are the feasts of the LORD, even holy convocations, which ye shall proclaim in their seasons. In
the fourteenth day of the first month at even is the
LORD'S passover.

Leviticus 23:4-5

THE FIRST IN ORDER OF THE
seven solemn feasts is the Feast of Passover. Symbolically it
typifies the foundation of the full accomplishment of God's
plan of salvation for sinners. Here in Leviticus 23 it is merely
mentioned in one verse. However, we are not left in ignorance
or doubt as to its meaning. In Leviticus, Moses simply lists it
as first among God's appointed feasts. However, it is fully presented in Exodus 12.

When the book of Exodus commences, Israel is a nation in
bondage and slavery. For more than four hundred years the
people were in Egypt under the tyranny of a pharaoh who
knew not Joseph (Exodus 1:8). They had increased abundantly
in number and became exceedingly mighty in strength and
influence. This growing strength of the Israelites caused
Pharaoh to become apprehensive, so he issued some severe
decrees whereby they would ultimately become extinct. First,
he made their lives bitter with rigorous tasks as slaves. That
was followed by an edict with the highest authority that every
son born of an Israelite should be killed (1:10-22). The firstborn
were condemned to die.

But God intervened, saved the life of the baby Moses, and
prepared him to lead Israel out of the Egyptian bondage. Then
God completely reversed the edict of Pharaoh by His own
edict of counteraction: "And all the firstborn in the land of Egypt

25

shall die" (11:5). Death was coming to the land of Egypt but not at the hand of Pharaoh. God was in control. He had made an unconditional covenant with Abraham and confirmed it with Isaac and Jacob. He had plans for the children of Israel that could not be abrogated.

The sentence of death had been decreed, and rightly so. Sin and death are inseparably linked together. (See Genesis 2:17; Jeremiah 31:30; Ezekiel 18:4; Romans 5:12; 6:23; James 1:15.) Since God is eternally righteous and cannot change, the sentence of death must be carried out. Because of His unconditional covenant with Abraham, Isaac, and Jacob, He must provide deliverance of His people from that death sentence. But it must be on a righteous basis. Now it is God's prerogative to provide the means whereby He can justify the guilty sinner and at the same time satisfy His own holy demands on righteous grounds.

It is at this point that Israel as a nation is first introduced to the striking and significant title of "lamb." The word *lamb* appears first in Scripture in Genesis 22:8, but not until it is used in Exodus 12 do we get a glimpse of its fullest doctrinal and prophetical importance. The following are just a few of the salient and significant points about the lamb as recorded in Exodus 12.

First, the lamb must be *selected*. "Speak ye unto all the congregation of Israel, saying, In the tenth day of this month they shall take to them every man a lamb, according to the house of their fathers, a lamb for a house" (Exodus 12:3). An Israelite might have suggested a plan whereby death could be avoided, but only the sovereign and holy God could make the choice. The sinner at his best could never know the demands of the holy and righteous God because "the natural man receiveth not the things of the Spirit of God: for they are foolish-ness unto him: neither can he know them, because they are spiritually discerned" (1 Corinthians 2:14). The issue here is the big difference between life and death. The sinner being spiritually dead does not know what real life is. God only is the giver and sustainer of life, therefore He must make the selection.

That the lamb pointed to the person of Jesus Christ is unques-tionable, and only God Himself could foresee this. In the first direct reference to the lamb in Scripture, Abraham said to Isaac, "God will provide himself a lamb" (Genesis 22:8). The lamb was God's choice before ever the nation Israel was born. Jesus Christ was "the Lamb slain from the foundation of the world" (Revelation 13:8) and "foreordained before the foundation of the world" (1 Peter 1:19-20).

Second, the lamb must be *spotless.* "Your lamb shall be without blemish, a male" (Exodus 12:5). Here we see the perfect type of our Lord Jesus Christ. The Holy Spirit guided the apostle Peter in using that identical description of God's lamb when he wrote, "Forasmuch as ye know that ye were not redeemed with corruptible things, as silver and gold from your vain conversation received by tradition from your fathers; But with the precious blood of Christ, as of a Lamb without blemish and without spot" (1 Peter 1:18-19).

Had there been one flaw in Jesus Christ He would have been unfit as a sacrifice for sin. But He was God's perfect lamb. He knew no sin (2 Corinthians 5:21); He did no sin (1 Peter 2:22); in Him was no sin (1 John 3:5). He prayed that others would be forgiven, but He never prayed for forgiveness for Himself because in Him there were no sins needing to be confessed and forgiven. He never dissuaded anyone from believing that He was sinless. He never offered a sacrifice for Himself, but He did offer Himself a sinless sacrifice for the sins of the world.

The Passover lamb was to be kept from the tenth day of the month until the fourteenth day of the month for careful scrutiny (Exodus 12:3,6). It was a time of testing. The life of our Lord Jesus Christ was also a period of testing. By His life He could not save one sinner, but His sinless life was necessary to His substitutionary death for sinners. If the slightest deviation from holiness were to be seen in Him, He could be neither the anti-type of the Passover lamb nor the Savior for us sinners. His earthly life provided ample time and sufficient opportunity for a detailed, critical examination of Him.

The life of our Lord had to meet the highest standards of God the Father. Abraham said, "God will provide himself a lamb" (Genesis 22:8). The Father had to be satisfied, and He most certainly was, for He testified, "This is my beloved Son, in whom I am well pleased" (Matthew 3:17). Heaven approved Him.

Then, too, Christ would be assiduously watched by Satan and demons. But they were never able to charge Him with sin. The demons testified, "I know thee, who thou art, the Holy One of God" (Mark 1:24). Satan and the demons recognized both His deity and sinlessness. (In this they are better theologians than are some ministers and teachers of religion.) Satan witnessed God's spotless lamb in the wilderness confrontation (Matthew 4:1-11).

Judas, who walked with our Lord closely for three years and betrayed Him, testified, "I have sinned in that I have betrayed the innocent blood" (Matthew 27:4). In this closing scene of the life of Judas, his confession and his effort toward repentance and restitution were too late to benefit him, but the recorded

28

testimony he gave of our Lord was both timely and timeless. He knew well that Jesus Christ's character was flawless.

Both the Roman governor and his wife bore witness to the perfection of God's lamb. Pilate said, "I find no fault in this man" (Luke 23:4), and, "I am innocent of the blood of this just person" (Matthew 27:24). His wife added, "Have thou nothing to do with that just man" (Matthew 27:19). Upon Pontius Pilate lay the grave responsibility of issuing or withholding the death penalty, and although notorious for corruption, he could speak no ill of Jesus Christ.

Third, the lamb must be *slain*. God's redemption centered in the Passover lamb. After the lamb was examined thoroughly to prove it was flawless, it had to be slain and its blood applied. The Passover lamb slain represents the death of our Lord Jesus Christ. While the New Testament is in the Old Testament concealed, the Old is in the New revealed. The prophet Isaiah identified the slain lamb to be a man when he wrote, "He is brought as a lamb to the slaughter, and as a sheep before her shearers is dumb, so he openeth not his mouth" (Isaiah 53:7).

With unmistakable clarity John the baptist identified Him when he said of Christ, "Behold the lamb of God, which taketh away the sin of the world" (John 1:29). But it was to the apostle Paul that the Holy Spirit revealed the Old Testament Passover lamb to be Jesus Christ when he said, "For even Christ our passover is sacrificed for us" (1 Corinthians 5:7). Undoubtedly many lambs were slain on that Passover night in Egypt, yet Exodus 12 does not speak of "lambs" in the plural number, always in the singular (see "it" in verse 6).

We cannot stress too strongly the fact that the lamb must be slain. The living lamb without any defect at all could not atone for man's sin. The life of our Lord Jesus Christ, though sinless and spotless, could not atone for sin. Nor does the mere fact

that God loves sinners atone for sin. We are not saved by the love of God nor by the life of the Son of God, but by the blood of the lamb of God. The clear definition of the Christian gospel declares "how that Christ died for our sins according to the Scriptures" (1 Corinthians 15:3). The holy Scriptures tell it all: the lamb must be slain. "Forasmuch as ye know that ye were not redeemed with corruptible things, as silver and gold, from your vain conversation received by tradition from your fathers; But with the precious blood of Christ, as of a lamb without blemish and without spot" (1 Peter 1:18-19).

In Revelation 5 the one sitting upon the throne held in His hand a book (or scroll). That book contained the title deed to the earth. An angel proclaimed with a loud voice, "Who is worthy to open the book and to loose the seals thereof?" or, "Who qualifies to claim the title deed to the earth?" A search found no one in heaven, on earth, or in the spirit world of the doomed capable of claiming the right to the earth. John wept when there was not one who could respond. As he wept, one of the elders said, "Weep not: behold, the Lion of the tribe of Judah, the Root of David, hath prevailed to open the book, and to loose the seven seals thereof" (5:3-5). John said he turned toward the throne to see the Lion, but there was no lion. He did see the chief Son of the royal tribe of Judah, but He appeared "a Lamb as it had been slain" (5:6). There in heaven stood God's lamb with the marks of death upon Him, as He had been slain. Yes, the lamb must be slain.

When the crucified and risen Lord stood forth as the lamb that had been slain, the twenty-four elders (representatives of all the redeemed) "sung a new song, saying, Thou art worthy to take the book, and to open the seals thereof: for Thou wast slain, and hast redeemed us to God by thy blood out of every kindred, and tongue, and people, and nation" (Revelation 5:8-

9). In Revelation 7 another large company of redeemed people of all nations and languages appears. They are the tribulation saints who will be saved after the rapture of the church, "and have washed their robes, and made them white in the blood of the Lamb" (7:9-14).

These words of Scripture show clearly that in past eternity the sovereign and omniscient God foreknew man's ruin by sin and his redemption by the divine provision in the blood sacrifice of "the Lamb slain from the foundation of the world" (13:8).

Fourth, the lamb must be a *substitute*. When God selected the Passover lamb, He intended the death of the lamb to be a substitute in the place of others, or, in the stead of others. The necessity of a substitute was clearly demonstrated from the moment sin entered the human race. The aprons of fig leaves Adam and Eve made for themselves could not cover their sin and shame in the eyes of a holy God. So God provided the substitute. "Unto Adam also and to his wife did the LORD God make coats of skins, and clothed them" (Genesis 3:21). Cain and Abel brought their offerings to the Lord. Abel brought a slain lamb as his substitute, "And the LORD had respect unto Abel and to his offering: But unto Cain and to his offering he had not respect" (4:3-5).

The biblical doctrine of substitution is a basic teaching of Christianity. "But God commendeth his love toward us, in that, while we were yet sinners, Christ died for us" (Romans 5:8). "Christ died for our sins according to the Scriptures" (1 Corinthians 15:3). "Christ loved the church and gave himself for it" (Ephesians 5:25). "The Son of God, who loved me, and gave himself for me" (Galatians 2:20). "Who gave himself for our sins" (Galatians 1:4). Our Lord Himself said, "Even as the Son of man came not to be ministered unto, but to minister, and to give his life a ransom for many" (Matthew 20:28).

31

There are other passages dealing with the substitutionary aspects of the Passover lamb but none more pronounced than Paul's statement, "For even Christ our Passover is sacrificed for us" (1 Corinthians 5:7). Any sinner may be a partaker of Christ the Passover lamb if he or she will but confess the fact of personal sin and receive Christ as the one and only redeemer. It is a personal and an individual matter. The sinner must believe as did Paul and personalize it as he did when he said, "The Son of God loved me, and gave himself for me" (Galatians 2:20).

Louis Goldberg summarized it well when he wrote, "All Israel knew that the Passover commemorated a deliverance from physical bondage. However, the Lord also intended that through that deliverance and the subsequent revelation at Mt. Sinai the nation should learn the meaning of spiritual redemption. As God was sensitive to the cry of the physically afflicted, so He was also sensitive to those in spiritual bondage. Just as the Israelites were to be free from slavery to their Egyptian taskmasters, so the people of God were to be free from the chains of sin. The term 'Lord's Passover' was used to describe not only the shedding of blood to release the Israelites from Egypt, but also thereafter to refer to the shedding of blood as a necessity to release them from the penalty of sin as indicated in the Levitical system."

Fifth, the blood of the lamb must be *sprinkled.* "And they shall take of the blood, and strike it on the two side posts and on the upper doorpost of the houses" (Exodus 12:7). In both Testaments numerous passages speak of sprinkling the blood. The terms *strike* and *sprinkle* convey the same thought, namely, "applying." The lamb's blood must be slain and the blood shed, but it had to be applied personally by faith. God said,

"And the blood shall be to you for a token upon the houses where ye are: and when I see the blood, I will pass over you, and the plague shall not be upon you to destroy you, when I smite the land of Egypt" (Exodus 12:13).

It was not enough that a Hebrew father killed the lamb. God's instruction to apply the blood of the lamb to the door-posts had to be obeyed by faith in His word. God said, "When I see the blood, I will pass over you." The blood was for their protection; God's assuring word was for their peace of mind. They had the assurance that they were safe because God had promised it. The angel of death would pass over every house where the blood was applied on the doorpost. The sprinkled blood sanctified that house. (See Leviticus 8:30; 9:12,18.) New Testament believers are said to be "elect according to the fore-knowledge of God the Father, through sanctification of the Spirit, unto obedience and sprinkling of the blood of Jesus Christ: Grace unto you and peace, be multiplied" (1 Peter 1:2). When we by faith apply the finished work of the Lord Jesus Christ to our hearts, we too have the assurance of eternal salvation and security.

The Passover marked the new beginning in Israel's calendar. God had said, "This month shall be unto the beginning of months: It shall be the first month of the year to you" (Exodus 12:2). Even so, when a believing sinner can say in sincerity and in truth, "Christ my Passover is sacrificed for me," he is born again. It is the beginning of months. "Therefore if any man be in Christ, he is a new creature: old things are passed away; behold all things are become new" (2 Corinthians 5:17). When our Lord said to Nicodemus, "Ye must be born again," he responded with the question, "How can these things be?" (John 3:3,7,9). Jesus answered and said unto him, "Art thou a master of Israel, and knowest not these things?" (3:10). The inference is clear. The trained Israelite should have known all about God's calendar.

My father and mother had seven children. My sister, the eldest and first to arrive, was a firstborn. I was the second to arrive, but I too was a firstborn. As a matter of fact, each of the seven was a firstborn. If we did not have the Word of God to teach us, this would be very confusing. The Bible teaches that there is more than one birth. The firstborn is under the sentence of death because of the sin of the first Adam. "Wherefore, as by one man sin entered into the world, and death by sin; and so death passed upon all men, for that all have sinned" (Romans 5:12).

By virtue of our first birth we are spiritually dead (Ephesians 2:1) and therefore need to be "second born." The second birth is not physical but spiritual; it is from above. We must be "second born" because we were not born right when we were "first born." The lamb was slain to redeem the "firstborn." When we receive the Passover lamb we experience the second birth into the family of the last Adam. Then we are born of God (John 1:13) and bought by God (1 Corinthians 6:19-20), the price being "the precious blood of Christ, as of a lamb without blemish and without spot" (1 Peter 1:18-19).

Now God's prophetic calendar comes into clear focus. The institution of the Passover in Exodus 12 pointed forward to the day God's lamb would provide a new beginning for us sinners. Life does not begin when we are "first born," which, in reality, is the beginning of death. Life begins when we are "second born." The day we are born again the past is blotted out. Hezekiah testified in his prayer to God, "Thou hast cast all my sins behind thy back" (Isaiah 38:17). The psalmist David wrote, "As far as the east is from the west, so far hath he removed our transgressions from us" (Psalm 103:12). The prophet Micah wrote, "Thou wilt cast all their sins into the depths of the sea" (Micah 7:19). God kept the first appointment on schedule as He wrote it in His prophetic calendar. The Passover is the foundation of the seven feasts. Our salvation is the starting point.

A point of interest in our present study is the fact that when there are two brothers in one family the elder, or firstborn, is the unbeliever whom God rejects, and the younger, or second born, is the believer whom God accepts. This principle is observed first in Cain and Abel. Cain the firstborn rejected God's plan of salvation and became the first murderer. Abel the second born accepted God's way of salvation and was accepted by God (Genesis 4:1-9; Hebrews 11:4; 1 John 3:10-12).

Abraham's first two children were boys. Ishmael the firstborn was conceived after the flesh and was rejected by God. Isaac, who was born second, was conceived supernaturally by the Spirit and became heir of the promises of God (Genesis 16:1-6; 17:18-19; 21:1-12; Galatians 4:22-31).

When Isaac was forty years old he married Rebekah. Their first children were twin boys whom they named Esau and Jacob. Before the sons were born, God revealed to Rebekah that "the elder (firstborn) shall serve the younger (second born" (Genesis 25:19-23). God made a sovereign choice when He rejected the firstborn and accepted the one born second (Romans 9:10-14 cf. Malachi 1:1-3).

Joseph had two sons, Ephraim and Manasseh. Manasseh was the firstborn, Ephraim was second born (Genesis 46:20). It was Joseph's desire that Manasseh, the firstborn and elder of the two brothers, should receive the blessing. But God would not have it that way. He guided Jacob in pronouncing the blessing upon Ephraim the second born (48:1,8-20).

We are all firstborn, that is, we had our first birth else we would not be here. But having been born with Adam's sin nature we are under the sentence of death. We need a second birth, a new birth. We must be born again by the power of the Holy Spirit. Our first birth cannot bring us to God. When we receive the Lord Jesus Christ, God's Passover lamb, we receive eternal life, God's very own life. The death of our Lord Jesus Christ at Calvary is where it all began.

Have you trusted Christ as your personal Savior? Have you been born again? Life begins at the second birth. According to God's calendar it is "the beginning of months: It shall be the first month of the year to you." Come to God's feast of Passover, partake of God's lamb, and you will pass from death to everlasting life (John 5:24).

2

The Feast of Unleavened Bread

God's Provision for Sanctification

Leviticus 23:6-8

The gospel of the grace of God, with all that follows in its train, may be found in Leviticus. This is the glorious attraction to every reader who feels himself a sinner. The New Testament has about forty references to its various ordinances. The likeness between type and antitype is never accidental. Leviticus contains a full system of truth exhibiting sin and the sinner, grace and the Saviour.

ANDREW A. BONAR

And on the fifteenth day of the same month is the feast of unleavened bread unto the LORD: seven days ye must eat unleavened bread. In the first day ye shall have an holy convocation: ye shall do no servile work therein. But ye shall offer an offering made by fire unto the LORD seven days: in the seventh day is an holy convocation: ye shall do no servile work therein.

Leviticus 23:6-8

THE SECOND FEAST, NAMELY Unleavened Bread, began the day following the Passover. The Passover lamb was slain on the fourteenth day of the month, at sunset (Leviticus 23:6). The fifteenth day began immediately after sunset, so that there was actually no lapse of time between the first and second feasts. The two were so closely related in time that, in the New Testament, Passover is included in "the days of unleavened bread" (Matthew 26:2; Luke 22:1).

There is a vital truth in all of this. Passover was a one-day feast, and the slaying of the lamb was a single act. There were other one-day feasts. But these feasts of longer duration point to the outcome of those acts. Passover is the type of Christ's death, a one time, single act that never needs repeating, "For in that he died, he died unto sin once . . ."(Romans 6:10 cf. Hebrews 10:10-12). Passover tells us what the Lord Jesus Christ has done for us. Unleavened Bread presents a picture of the character of the believer's life after he has received Christ. No Israelite was saved by putting away the leaven; they put away the leaven because they were saved.

The Feast of Unleavened Bread was of seven days duration

39

(Leviticus 23:6; Numbers 28:17; Deuteronomy 16:1-4), one full week, a perfect period of time. As the Passover lamb is a type of Christ's death, the foundation of our union with God, so the seven day Feast of Unleavened Bread points to the character of the believer's walk, the ground of his communion with God. We must always be aware of the difference between our relationship with God and our fellowship with God. Faith in the blood of Christ is the final step in our redemption from the Godward side, but the command to Israel to eat bread with no leaven showed their responsibility as redeemed people. A holy life is the condition under which this new relationship with God is enjoyed.

Leaven here, as elsewhere in the Bible, is a symbol of evil, of moral corruption—always evil, only evil, carrying its putrifaction wherever it works. Each day of the week every trace of leaven had to be removed from every dwelling where the blood of the Passover lamb had been applied. The believer must not be satisfied with merely being saved by the blood of the lamb. A sweet and sacred communion must be cultivated between the redeemed ones and the Redeemer. No believer can enjoy salvation until the leaven is put away.

We repeat for emphasis that great principle concerning the two Testaments: "The New is in the Old concealed, the Old is in the New revealed." The type now becomes clear. The apostle Paul wrote, "Purge out therefore the old leaven, that ye may be a new lump, as ye are unleavened. For even Christ our passover is sacrificed for us: Therefore let us keep the feast, not with old leaven, neither with the leaven of malice and wickedness; but with the unleavened bread of sincerity and truth" (1 Corinthians 5:7-8). As far as God is concerned, the Passover (death of Christ) met every righteous demand against sin. However, the Feast of Unleavened Bread marks the beginning of the believing sinner's fellowship with God, which is based on practical holiness.

All of this is markedly significant from the doctrinal point of view. The Passover sets forth the doctrine of salvation. Unleavened Bread presents the doctrine of sanctification, the two doctrines being vitally and inseparably joined together. Moreover, there is a logical progression in the order of the two. Sanctification follows naturally after salvation. I have just pointed out in 1 Corinthians 5:7-8 how forcefully Paul applies to the lives of Christians this great principle involved in these symbols. He is telling us what God meant when He commanded the Israelites to put away leaven. So let us pursue this pertinent and personal doctrine of sanctification, remembering its place in the order of the feasts of the Lord.

The nouns *saint* and *sanctification* and the verb *sanctify* have in them a common Greek root. The Greek word *hagiazo,* translated "to sanctify," means "to separate, set apart." For example, the Scriptures tell us that God sanctified the seventh day (Genesis 2:3) and the tabernacle (Leviticus 8:10). Many other objects in the Old Testament are likewise said to be sanctified. None of these inanimate objects are capable of sinning. They are amoral, therefore they are neither moral nor immoral. They were objects that were to be set apart for holy purposes.

Frequently in the Bible God's people are called saints, a common designation in the New Testament for those who have been redeemed through faith in Jesus Christ. The term is used of all believers and is therefore not applied merely to those persons whose lives are characterized by exceptional acts of holiness or saintliness. For example, in the church at Corinth there were carnal Christians whose behavior was characterized by sins of almost every description, but because they were born again they are said to be "sanctified in Christ Jesus, called to be saints" (1 Corinthians 1:2). They were unsaintly saints, therefore Paul exhorted them to "purge out the old leaven."

There are three steps (or stages) in the believer's sanctification:

1. *Positional Sanctification.* When any individual accepts the gospel, that person is at once set apart by the Holy Spirit, the divine agent in sanctification. "Elect according to the foreknowledge of God the Father through sanctification of the Spirit . . ."(1 Peter 1:2). "But we are bound to give thanks alway to God for you, brethren beloved of the Lord, because God hath from the beginning chosen you to salvation through sanctification of the Spirit and belief of the truth" (2 Thessalonians 2:13). "And such were some of you: but ye are washed, but ye are sanctified, but ye are justified in the name of the Lord Jesus, and by the Spirit of our God" (1 Corinthians 6:11). Positional sanctification is the standing of every child of God. We have been set apart by the holy God in order that we might live a holy life.

2. *Practical Sanctification.* This is the emphasis in the Feast of Unleavened Bread. In God's calendar, sanctification follows salvation. "Ye are sanctified," therefore be in practice what you are positionally. "For this is the will of God, even your sanctification, that ye should abstain from fornication" (1 Thessalonians 4:3). "For God hath not called us unto uncleanness, but unto holiness" (4:7).

Positional sanctification is vicarious, that is, it is imputed to us at the time of salvation. However, practical sanctification is not vicarious; it cannot be transferred from one person to another. It comes to each individual by means of a learning process. The Holy Spirit is our teacher and the Word of God is the instrument He uses. Our Lord said, "Now ye are clean through the word which I have spoken unto you" (John 15:3).

He prayed to the Father, "Sanctify them through thy truth: thy word is truth" (John 17:17). As we obey the teachings in the Holy Scriptures we are setting ourselves apart to the purpose for which God set us apart when He saved us.

3. *Perfect Sanctification.* In both the Old and New Testaments we read, "Ye shall be holy; for I the LORD your God am holy" (Leviticus 11:44-45; 19:2; 20:7; 1 Peter 1:16). In the Sermon on the Mount our Lord said to His disciples, "Be ye therefore perfect, even as your Father which is in heaven is perfect" (Matthew 5:48). Perfect in holiness is the ultimate in sanctification. God only is perfectly holy. In this life we Christians cannot attain to perfect sanctification. However, true believers in Christ realize the responsibility enjoined upon them.

If we Christians cannot reach perfection, why then did our Lord say to His disciples, "Be ye therefore perfect, even as your Father which is in heaven is perfect"? He was telling them that perfection is the goal of every believer which, even though it is not attainable in this life, we must strive day by day to improve in practical holiness. We must put away the leaven of lying, jealousy, hatred, gossip, hypocrisy, selfishness. Because the Adamic nature remains a part of us, temptations will arise every day.

But there is awaiting every child of God a time when we all shall be perfectly sanctified. "To the end he may stablish your hearts unblameable in holiness before God, even our Father, at the coming of our Lord Jesus Christ with all his saints" (1 Thessalonians 3:13). "When he shall appear, we shall be like him; for we shall see him as he is" (1 John 3:2). When our Lord returns, "we shall be changed" (1 Corinthians 15:51), sanctified "wholly," that is, complete in every part of our beings.

God contemplated much more in the death of Christ than the mere pardon of our sins. When He redeemed Israel from

Egyptian bondage, His purpose was that His people should be delivered from the unholy practices of the old life. The principle of sin will always be a part of each of us, but the practice of sin must not continue in us. Salvation from the penalty of sin must be followed by sanctification from the practice of sin. Christ "gave himself for our sins, that he might deliver us from this present evil world, according to the will of God and our Father" (Galatians 1:4). "He died for all, that they which live should not henceforth live unto themselves, but unto him which died for them, and rose again" (2 Corinthians 5:15). The larger purpose of the Feast of Unleavened Bread is seen when we consider its prophetic fulfillment: "Purge out therefore the old leaven, that ye may be a new lump, as ye are unleavened. For even Christ our passover is sacrificed for us: Therefore let us keep the feast, not with the old leaven, neither with the leaven of malice and wickedness; but with the unleavened bread of sincerity and truth" (1 Corinthians 5:7-8).

On several occasions our Lord used leaven in His teaching, showing it to be a principle of evil of which every believer should beware.

1. *The Leaven of Deceit.* "He began to say unto his disciples first of all, Beware ye of the leaven of the Pharisees, which is hypocrisy" (Luke 12:1). The word *hypocrisy* (Greek, *hupokrisis*) denotes playacting. Before electricity was discovered, which brought with it the many and varied sound devices used today, Greek and Roman actors wore large masks covering the head and face. Concealed in them was a mechanical device for controlling the volume and intonation of the voice. *Hypocrite* (Greek, *hupokrites*) was the term used for a stage actor.

The professing Christian who merely plays the part of a believer in Christ is a hypocrite. Our Lord condemned mere externalism in religion, doing good deeds "before men to be seen of them" (Matthew 6:1). He said that hypocrites give to the needy "that they may have glory of men" (6:2-4). Hypocrites pray that they may be seen and heard of men (6:5-6). Hypocrites fast "that they may appear unto men to fast" (6:16-18). On one occasion Christ spoke directly to the Pharisees and said, "Ye hypocrites, well did Esaias prophesy of you, saying, This people draweth nigh unto me with their mouth, and honoureth me with their lips; but their heart is far from me" (Matthew 15:7-8 cf. Isaiah 29:13). "Then came his disciples, and said unto him, Knowest thou that the Pharisees were offended, after they heard this saying?" (Matthew 15:12). Of course they were offended. They had fallen into a lifestyle of deceit, playacting, pretending outwardly to being what they were not. A false impression is the leaven of deceit. (Read Matthew 23:1-29.)

A hypocrite, then, is any person who knowingly and willfully pretends. I am not a hypocrite if I do not live up to my potential or reach the goals I set. Even if I fail to carry out my responsibilities, I cannot be guilty of hypocrisy. Pretending to reach my goals when I have not is hypocrisy. Pretending to have carried out my responsibilities when I have not done so is hypocrisy (1 John 1:6). Pretending to love my wife as Christ loved the church when I do not is hypocrisy (Ephesians 5:25). All pretense is hypocrisy. It is the sin that keeps us from "the unleavened bread of sincerity and truth" (1 Corinthians 5:8).

The Pharisees were a religious sect who concerned themselves in the matter of abiding within the letter of the law. The name Pharisee means separatist. Saul of Tarsus was of the Pharisaic school (Philippians 3:5). The Pharisees believed they were more righteous than others, hence to them their attitude of superiority was justified. Read the prayer of the Pharisee in Luke 18:10-12 and you will see the Pharisees' heart. They were enemies of the Lord Jesus Christ and murmured (Luke 15:2) and took counsel against Him (Matthew 12:14). Emphasizing their pretences and outward ostentation to piety, they significantly omitted the weightier matters of the law and became avaricious, hypocritical, and sensual (Matthew 23:13-33). Against them our Lord pronounced seven awful "woes," calling them "serpents" and a "generation of vipers," hardly able to escape the damnation of hell. Beware of the leaven of the Pharisees.

2. *The Leaven of Defilement.* To defile means to render unholy, unclean. It is the leaven of moral corruption. Our Lord warned against it when He charged His disciples, "Take heed, beware of the leaven of Herod" (Mark 8:15). Herod was a ruthless politician who ordered all children in Bethlehem, two years old and under, to be slain (Matthew 14:1-12). Luke wrote about "all the evils which Herod had done" (Luke 3:19), and how he "vexed the church" (Acts 12:1). The immoral lifestyle of Herod is evidenced in his desire to kill our Lord (Luke 13:31-32) and in his adultery with Herodias, his half-brother Philip's wife (Matthew 14:1-3). The leaven of Herod is the leaven of worldliness.

The leaven of moral corruption in the church at Corinth was no secret. When Paul used the word *leaven* in 1 Corinthians 5 it was in direct relation to immorality in that local assembly (5:1-6). He follows immediately with the exhortation, "Purge out therefore the old leaven, that ye may be a new lump, as ye are unleavened" (5:7). He was telling them to get rid of the old leaven (that evil practice) because they really were without leaven (positionally). I have already pointed out the fact that the Christians in the church at Corinth were said to be sanctified (set apart) positionally so that they were positionally "unleavened." But the leaven of moral corruption needed to be

46

put away from their lives. "Let us cleanse ourselves from all filthiness of the flesh and spirit, perfecting holiness in the fear of God" (2 Corinthians 7:1). "And let every one that nameth the name of Christ depart from iniquity" (2 Timothy 2:19).

3. *The Leaven of Doctrinal Deficiency.* When our Lord said, "Take heed and beware of the leaven of the Pharisees and of the Sadducees," He meant "the doctrine of the Pharisees and of the Sadducees" (Matthew 16:6, 11-12). The Pharisees taught that a person was religious and could please God if he appeared right outwardly, even though his heart might be filled with malice, greed, envy, jealousy, lust, and hate. The Sadducees taught "that there is no resurrection" (Matthew 22:23). They were the existentialists of their day. To them life consisted merely of the present, of that which one could see, touch, and taste. They were the intellectual freethinkers who ignored the doctrines of the Scriptures and the power of God (22:29). Apparently there were Sadducees in the assembly in Corinth (1 Corinthians 15:12). Denying the fact of the resurrection was the leading deficiency in their creed. That was the leaven of the Sadducees.

In the province of Galatia the leaven of doctrinal deficiency had appeared in a different form. Many of the believers, newborn and spiritually immature, came under the influence of legalistic teachers. Were these Christians, having been justified by grace through faith, under the law? So the legalizers would have them believe. Paul handled the problem well in several places in the Epistle (see Galatians 2:19-21; 3:1-3; 3:25-26; 4:4-6; 4:9-13). He concluded that if any person, Jew or Gentile, accepts salvation through faith in Christ, and then puts himself again under the law, he behaves as if he were still unsaved. Then in chapter 5 he nails down his conclusion by warning them that "a little leaven leaveneth the whole lump" (5:1-8).

Again, leaven is an evil principle. Beware of the leaven of the Sadducees.

As we conclude our study of the Feast of Unleavened Bread, we are faced with a most pertinent and practical question. How can we, as God's redeemed children, remove the leaven from our lives? How can we practice holiness seven days of every week? This is a problem with which we all have struggled.

Consider again 1 Corinthians 5:7-8: "For even Christ our passover is sacrificed for us: Therefore let us keep the feast." The "feast" here has reference to the Feast of Unleavened Bread. Remember, the New is in the Old concealed. Look again at the Lord's description of the feast in Exodus 12.

Speaking of the lamb, the Lord said, "And they shall eat the flesh in that night, roast with fire, and unleavened bread: and with bitter herbs they shall eat it" (Exodus 12:8). The Israelites were saved by the blood of the lamb, and now they are instructed to feast on the lamb. Moses followed this instruction with clear statements that only those who had been redeemed by the blood could share in the feast (12:43-51). No foreigner or stranger was permitted to eat the feast.

We have been reminded repeatedly that the lamb is a type of our Lord Jesus Christ. He is the lamb of God who was slain and sacrificed for us. What then did Paul mean when he said, "For even Christ our passover was sacrificed for us: Therefore let us keep the feast" (1 Corinthians 5:7-8)? He is telling those of us who have been redeemed by Christ's blood that we must feast on the lamb.

One of the prescribed ministries of the Holy Spirit is to draw the born again ones to the lamb. Our Lord Himself said that when the Holy Spirit comes, "He shall testify of me" (John 15:26), and "He shall glorify me" (John 16:14). A Spirit-controlled Christian will "keep the feast" as he feeds on the Lord

Jesus Christ on all seven days of the week (Exodus 12:15; Leviticus 23:6).

What does it mean to feed on Christ? Our Lord said, "Verily, verily, I say unto you, Except ye eat the flesh of the Son of man, and drink his blood, ye have no life in you. Whoso eateth my flesh, and drinketh my blood, hath eternal life; and I will raise him up at the last day" (John 6:53-54). Now you may be asking, "What did our Lord mean by these words?"

In the first place, He was not referring to the Lord's Supper. While it is true that He did institute the Lord's Supper at the last Passover and Feast of Unleavened Bread, His remarks as to eating His flesh and drinking His blood did not refer to that Supper. (See Matthew 26:13-29.) It would be a gross error for anyone to assume that in John 6:53-54 Christ taught that those who do not partake of the Lord's Supper would be cut off from eternal life.

In the second place, our Lord was not speaking literally of eating His flesh and drinking His blood. When He took the bread and blessed and brake and gave it to His disciples and said, "Take, eat; this is my body" (Matthew 26:26), He was definitely not using the words "body" and "blood" literally. When he spoke of eating His flesh and drinking His blood, He used those terms symbolically, figuratively. Just as food and drink sustain us physically, so Christ sustains us spiritually. Feeding on Christ denotes that close communion with Him which strengthens and sustains the believer.

But how do we feed on Christ? His great discourse on the bread of life in John 6:22-63 followed His miraculous feeding of the five thousand (6:1-14). No one to this day can understand how the loaves and fishes were multiplied to feed the five thousand. Suffice it to say the people were fed. Moreover, the feeding of that crowd was not merely a physical necessity, but a spiritual figure as well. Following the miracle, the Lord Jesus said, "I am the bread of life: he that cometh to me shall never hunger; and he that believeth on me shall never thirst" (John 6:35). Just as we receive Christ for our salvation, so we must feed on Him for practical sanctification.

Our Lord concluded His discourse on the bread of life by stating how we can feed on Him. He said, "It is the Spirit that quickeneth; the flesh profiteth nothing: the words that I speak unto you, they are spirit, and they are life" (John 6:63). Six times, once in each verse (6:51-56), He speaks of eating His flesh. Obviously, He had no reference to His literal body of flesh because He said in conclusion, "The flesh profiteth nothing."

"The words that I speak unto you, they are spirit, and they are life." Now we know that Christ Himself is the Word incarnate (John 1:1; 1 John 1:1; Revelation 19:13), but here in John 6:63 He is referring to the Word inscripturated, the written Word. He used the plural *words*. The Scriptures are life-giving and life-sustaining. He said, "Verily, verily, I say unto you, He that heareth my word, and believeth on him that sent me, hath everlasting life, and shall not come into condemnation; but is passed from death unto life" (John 5:24). The Word of God has power to bring any sinner out from spiritual death into spiritual life (Hebrews 4:12).

The Word of God has power to save the sinner, and it has power to sustain and strengthen the Christian. It is the milk (1 Peter 2:2) and meat (Hebrews 5:12-14) for the soul. The prophet testified, "Thy words were found, and I did eat them; and thy Word was unto me the joy and rejoicing of mine heart" (Jeremiah 15:16).

The Christian who neglects the daily reading and study of the Bible is passing by the means provided by God for his spiritual growth. The practical sanctification and spiritual development of the child of God are dependent upon the daily feeding on Christ through the written Word of God. We feed on the lamb when we feed on the Holy Scriptures. This is the meaning of the Feast of Unleavened Bread. Children of God, let us keep the feast.

It is essential to examine those Scriptures which point out the severe penalty which resulted from the discovery of leaven in a Hebrew's house. God had said, "Whosoever eateth that which is leavened, even that soul shall be cut off from the congregation of Israel, whether he be a stranger, or born in the land" (Exodus 12:19). To be cut off could mean either death or severance from the fellowship of God and of the people of God, or both.

Any form of sin will be forgiven if the sinning person confesses his sin to God. Abraham was a liar, but he was forgiven. Moses was a murderer, but he was forgiven. David was both a murderer and an adulterer, but he was forgiven. Peter, a profane man, denied the Lord, but he was forgiven. These all were saints who sinned but were forgiven.

However, there is a sin unto death for the believer who refuses to put evil out of his life (1 John 5:16). Of course, no Christian loses the eternal life he received when he was born again. What the Christian loses is physical life. A Christian may be cut off from this life for living after the flesh (Romans 8:13), for failing to bear fruit (John 15:2), for lying to the Holy Spirit (Acts 5:1-6), for murmuring against God (Numbers 16:41-49), or for engaging in moral evil (1 Corinthians 5:1-8). Let us come humbly to God, confess every known and secret sin, and purge out the old leaven.

51

3

The Feast of Firstfruits

God's Pledge of Security

Leviticus 23:9-14

Seen from the New Testament perspective, the Bible Feasts present a symbolic enactment of the divine drama of salvation, types pointing to the larger fulfillment in Christ the Saviour. No Christian can fully understand his own spiritual heritage without going back to the Jewish Feasts with their solemn rites and God-appointed observances.

VICTOR BUKSBAZEN

And the LORD spake unto Moses, saying, Speak
unto the children of Israel, and say unto them, When
ye be come into the land which I give unto you, and
shall reap the harvest thereof, then ye shall bring a
sheaf of the firstfruits of your harvest unto the priest:
And he shall wave the sheaf before the LORD, to be
accepted for you: on the morrow after the sabbath
the priest shall wave it. And ye shall offer that day
when ye wave the sheaf an he lamb without blemish
of the first year for a burnt offering unto the LORD.
And the meat offering thereof shall be two tenth
deals of fine flour mingled with oil, an offering made
by fire unto the LORD for a sweet savour: and the
drink offering thereof shall be of wine, the fourth
part of an hin. And ye shall eat neither bread, nor
parched corn, nor green ears, until the selfsame day
that ye have brought an offering unto your God: it
shall be a statute for ever throughout your generations in all your dwellings.

Leviticus 23:9-14

OUR STUDY TO THIS POINT HAS
brought to light the fact that these Old Testament feasts are
not restricted to national Israel. When the Scriptures of the Old
and New Testaments are studied together, it becomes clear that
there is a wider message of prophecy and salvation for both
Jew and Gentile.

Seen from the New Testament, these Jewish holy days present God's prophetic calendar pointing to their wider fulfillment
in the Lord Jesus Christ. The holy days in the calendar "are a

THE FIRST COMING OF CHRIST

shadow of things to come; but the body is of Christ" (Colossians 2:17). The reality is in Christ. The Christian can better understand his spiritual heritage by a careful study of the Old Testament.

Now it becomes clearer as to why God established a new calendar, changing the seventh month to the first. The six months in the year of the old calendar show man to be what he really is, a fallen child of the first Adam, hopelessly and helplessly separated from God. So God makes a fresh beginning. The first Adam brought sin and death; the last Adam brought righteousness and immortality. "For as in Adam all die, even so in Christ shall all be made alive" (1 Corinthians 15:22). When God blotted out those first six months and instituted the new calendar, He did it upon a new foundation: the Passover lamb. The apostle Paul wrote, "For other foundation can no man lay than that is laid, which is Jesus Christ" (1 Corinthians 3:11).

In the seven feasts in Leviticus 23 we are shown how God laid the foundation for all that was to follow. The slaying of God's Passover lamb at Calvary would be a fatal tragedy had He not risen from among the dead. The Feast of Firstfruits pointed to the next event in God's prophetic calendar following the death of the Lord Jesus Christ, namely, His resurrection from death and the tomb.

Before we examine the prophetic fulfillment in the Feast of Firstfruits, a word of explanation should be given as to why I consider it to be a separate feast. It is true that this third in the series of the seven feasts is intimately connected with the Feast of Passover and Unleavened Bread. Therefore a few writers have stated that the waving of the sheaf of firstfruits was an essential feature of the Feast of Unleavened Bread and is therefore not to be considered as a separate feast. It is likewise true that the Feast of Firstfruits was held at the same convocation as were those of the Passover and Unleavened Bread, but I believe it has so distinct and separate an application as to stand alone.

Passover was celebrated on the fourteenth day of the month. Unleavened Bread was held from the fifteenth to the twenty-second day of that same month, seven full days. Firstfruits began on the seventeenth day of that month, "on the morrow after the Sabbath." There was an obvious overlapping insofar as time was concerned. However each of the three feasts was designed to teach and emphasize a different doctrinal and practical truth.

Give careful attention to the words in verse 9: "And the LORD spake unto Moses, saying . . . " While the use of these words does not necessarily suggest a break in the narrational structure of the chapter, they do indicate a fresh spiritual division. A. J. Holiday has suggested that "here the Lord is only adding a further instruction as to something to be done in that week when His people arrived in Canaan. But a new subject altogether is being set forth in type by this additional ordinance, and it is therefore introduced by the distinctive words, 'And the LORD spake unto Moses.' "

One striking difference did exist between this third feast and the two which preceded it. While Passover and Unleavened Bread could be held in the wilderness during the journey from Egypt to Canaan (Numbers 9:1-11), Firstfruits and the feasts that followed could be celebrated only in the promised land after the children of Israel had possessed the land. The Lord had said, "When ye be come into the land which I give unto you, and shall reap the harvest thereof, then ye shall bring a sheaf of the firstfruits of your harvest unto the priest" (Leviticus 23:10). It would not be observed in the wilderness where grain could not be sown or harvested.

A further command from the Lord made it clear to the people that they were to possess the land and not merely live there. "And it shall be, when thou art come in into the land which the LORD thy God giveth thee for an inheritance, and possessest it, and dwellest therein; That thou shalt take of the first of all the fruit of the earth, which thou shalt bring of the land that the LORD thy God giveth thee, and shall put it in a basket, and shalt go unto the place which the LORD thy God shall choose to put his name there" (Deuteronomy 26:1-2). Israel had to be in the land possessing their possessions. There is a qualitative difference between owning something and possessing it. Too often we Christians do not possess and enjoy all that God has bestowed upon us.

What are the lessons to be learned from the Feast of Firstfruits? First, there is a lesson *stewardship*. "Speak unto the children of Israel, and say unto them, When ye be come into the land which I give unto you, and shall reap the harvest thereof, then ye shall bring a sheaf of the firstfruits of your harvest unto the priest: and he shall wave the sheaf before the LORD, to be accepted for you: on the morrow after the sabbath the priest shall wave it" (Leviticus 23:10-11). The Israelite was now in the place of plenty, the place of God's bountiful provision, "a land of wheat, and barley, and vines, and fig trees, and pomegranates; a land of olive oil, and honey" (Deuteronomy 8:8-9). Canaan was for Israel a place of plenty and prosperity.

This first lesson to be learned in the Feast of Firstfruits is the principle of divine ownership. God is the creator and sustainer of the earth and its contents; His people are His custodians, His caretakers, His stewards. "The earth is the LORD's, and the fulness thereof" (Psalm 24:1; 1 Corinthians 10:26,28). In this life we own nothing. "For we brought nothing into this world, and it is certain we can carry nothing out" (1 Timothy 6:7). A man can accumulate great wealth, but he cannot keep it. God might not take from me what I gather in this life, but one day He will take me from it. What God gave to Israel was not theirs to keep, but its custody was a trust to be held for God. "The silver is mine, and the gold is mine, saith the LORD of hosts" (Haggai 2:8). The meaning of this feature of the feast was clear. The first sheaves of the ripe harvest were to be presented to the Lord, thereby indicating that the entire harvest belonged to Him.

For the Christian the principle to be applied is plain, pertinent, and personal. God is telling us that the first and best belong to Him. He must have first place in our lives. All we are and have and ever hope to get belong to the Lord. "Honour the LORD with thy substance, and with the firstfruits of all thine increase" (Proverbs 3:9). "Seek ye first the kingdom of God, and his righteousness; and all these things shall be added unto you" (Matthew 6:33).

Before an Israelite was permitted to bake any bread for himself, he had to bring the first sheaf to be presented to the Lord. The command from the Lord to His people was clear on this point. "And ye shall eat neither bread, nor parched corn, nor green ears, until the selfsame day that ye have brought an offering unto your God: It shall be a statute for ever throughout your generations in all your dwellings" (Leviticus 23:14).

At once we can see why Israel had to possess the land before they could present to Jehovah its firstfruits. They could not give to Him what they did not have. Nor can the Christian offer to God what he does not possess. The Bible says that God has "blessed us with all spiritual blessings in heavenly places in Christ" (Ephesians 1:3), but until we appropriate these blessings, we have nothing to offer Him. We may gather in so-called worship services and take part in every form and ceremony prescribed for us and still have nothing acceptable to offer the Lord. Much that is called worship is not worship at all. It is impossible to give to God what we ourselves have never received.

One reason why God gave the land of Canaan to Israel was to give to the people something they could give back to Him. God remained the owner of the land even as He continues as sovereign owner of the universe He created. Let us keep before us at all times this principle of divine ownership. God has first claim upon us and all that we possess. Our first and best belong to Him at all times.

We come now to the larger lesson taught in the feast of firstfruits, namely, the *security* of the believer. Stewardship has to do with the believer's responsibility in this present life; security is associated with the resurrection and our future life.

God's prophetic calendar began with the Passover when He said, "This month shall be unto you the beginning of months: it shall be the first month of the year to you" (Exodus 12:2). We saw how the type was fulfilled in the death of our Lord, the true Passover lamb who was sacrificed for us (1 Corintians 5:7). And in that same Epistle to the Corinthians the apostle Paul shows the next event in God's prophetic calendar. The next event to follow logically after the death and burial of the Lord Jesus Christ was His resurrection from death and the grave. Remember that the New is in the Old concealed; the Old is in the New revealed. It is in the New Testament where we have the full and final revelation of the prophecy in the Feast of Firstfruits.

1 Corinthians 15 is a New Testament classic on the subject of the resurrection of Christ and of Christians. Here Paul's

argument is clear and convincing. Christ arose from the dead, and so all who believe in Christ will be raised. "Christ the firstfruits, afterward they that are Christ's at his coming" (1 Corinthians 15:23).

It was at the very time of these first three feasts that our Lord died at Calvary and rose again. "Now the first day of the feast of unleavened bread the disciples came to Jesus, saying unto him, Where wilt thou that we prepare for thee to eat the passover?" (Matthew 26:17). In Paul's declaration of the Christian gospel, the death, burial, and resurrection of our Lord Jesus Christ are joined together as one unit: "Moreover, brethren, I declare unto you the gospel . . . for I delivered unto you first of all that which I also received, how that Christ died for our sins according to the scriptures; And that he was buried, and that he rose again the third day according to the scriptures" (1 Corinthians 15:1,3-4). When the apostle wrote these words, Christ's death, burial, and resurrection were past history, but the order in which he arranged them follows the order of the first three feasts. The Passover lamb died and rose again.

When our Lord rose from the dead, He became the firstfruits of those believers who had died and of those believers who were yet to die. When the Israelites brought that first sheaf of grain and presented it to the Lord, it was given as a token, a pledge, a guarantee that the remainder of the harvest would follow. When Christ arose from the dead and ascended to the Father, He presented Himself as the firstfruits, the pledge and guarantee that the harvest would follow. And what might that harvest be? God's true children who likewise will be raised and brought into the Father's presence are that harvest. When God the Father accepted Christ after His resurrection, that acceptance guaranteed the eternal security of all believers. When Paul said, "He rose again the third day according to the scriptures," He most assuredly meant the Old Testament Scriptures including Leviticus 23:9-14).

Our eternal security as Christians does not depend upon ourselves, but upon the completed work of our Lord Jesus Christ. Look again at 1 Corinthians 15:1-4 and note that the gospel would be incomplete apart from our Lord's resurrection. Every saved person may have the assurance that he will be raised from the dead and brought into the presence of God the Father. The apostle expressed it so well when he wrote that Jesus our Lord "was delivered for our offences, and was raised again for our justification" (Romans 4:25).

There is further scriptural evidence in support of the Christian's security. "For we know that the whole creation groaneth and travaileth in pain together until now. And not only they, but ourselves also, which have the firstfruits of the Spirit, even we ourselves groan within ourselves, waiting for the adoption, to wit, the redemption of our body" (Romans 8:22-23). Here the apostle speaks of the future aspect of adoption, namely, the redemption of our bodies, which takes place at the coming of Christ when we shall be raised. The assurance of that final stage of our redemption is the indwelling of the Holy Spirit, called here "the firstfruits of the Spirit." While our risen Lord is in heaven, the Holy Spirit is on earth having taken a permanent residence in the body of every Christian. That is double security: Christ the firstfruits in heaven who is coming for us, and the firstfruits of the Holy Spirit in us to secure us until our Lord Jesus Christ comes back.

In ancient times it was a common practice for people to make, or purchase, a personal seal or signet. They would attach the seal to everything they bought and owned. The seal identified the object with its owner. The Bible teaches that the Holy

Spirit is the divine seal in the life of every redeemed person. "In whom also after that ye believed, ye were sealed with that Holy Spirit of promise, which is the earnest of our inheritance until the redemption of the purchased possession, unto the praise of his glory" (Ephesians 1:13-14). The word *earnest* means "down payment." The Holy Spirit has been given to us as the down payment, the guarantee that our resurrection will follow. "God hath also sealed us, and given the earnest of the Spirit in our hearts" (2 Corinthians 1:22). The firstruits of the Holy Spirit simply means that God is giving to His children the assurance that the harvest will follow. Our Lord gave that word of assurance when He said, "Because I live, ye shall live also" (John 14:19). "Now is Christ risen from the dead, and become the firstfruits of them that slept" (1 Corinthians 15:20).

A further truth of great magnitude must not be overlooked. The New Testament teaches that we Christians are in some way a part of the firstfruits. "Of his own will begat he us with the word of truth, that we should be a kind of firstfruits of his creatures" (James 1:18). The moment you and I became saved, we became firstfruits, meaning that we became the beginning of a harvest.

In the early 1920's a girl in her early teens received Christ as her Savior. Immediately she became a firstfruits, the beginning of a harvest. In 1927 that girl led me to the acceptance of Christ as my Savior, and I became a part of her harvest. Upon receiving Christ as my Savior, I too became a firstfruits and thereby the beginning of a harvest. In 1931 that same girl and I were married. In 1933 our first child was born. In 1938 I was privileged to lead him to receive Christ, and he became a firstfruits and the beginning of a harvest. In 1941 our second son was born and later he received Christ and became a firstfruits and the beginning of a harvest. You see, God saved us so that we should increase the harvest.

When Elsie led me to Christ she didn't have the faintest idea of the far-reaching effects of her witness. In 1982 our grandson went to Ethiopia as a firstfruits missionary so that now three generations of firstfruits continue to labor in the gospel to increase the harvest. Christian, you and I are firstfruits. Is there a harvest following us? What will the harvest be? "He that goeth forth and weepeth, bearing precious seed, shall doubtless come again with rejoicing, bringing his sheaves with him" (Psalm 126:6).

4

The Feast of Weeks or Pentecost

God's Promise of the Spirit

Leviticus 23:15-22

Considered as embracing the history of one month only, Leviticus may claim to be the most remarkable book in the Old Testament. Focalized into that one month is the whole discipline of life. In no spiritual sense is Leviticus an obsolete book. The wonder is that there are Christians who are willing to regard Leviticus as obsolete. Without this book Christ as revealed in the gospels would have been impossible, and without Christ Leviticus would have been impossible.

JOSEPH PARKER

And ye shall count unto you from the morrow after the sabbath, from the day that ye brought the sheaf of the wave offering; seven sabbaths shall be completed: Even unto the morrow after the seventh sabbath shall ye number fifty days; and ye shall offer a new meat offering unto the LORD. Ye shall bring out of your habitations two wave loaves of two tenth deals: they shall be of fine flour; they shall be baken with leaven; they are the firstfruits unto the LORD. And ye shall offer with the bread seven lambs without blemish of the first year, and one young bullock, and two rams: they shall be for a burnt offering unto the LORD, with their meat offering, and their drink offering, even an offering made by fire, of sweet savour unto the LORD. Then ye shall sacrifice one kid of the goats for a sin offering, and two lambs of the first year for a sacrifice of peace offerings. And the priest shall wave them with the bread of the firstfruits for a wave offering before the LORD, with the two lambs: they shall be holy to the LORD for the priest. And ye shall proclaim on the selfsame day, that it may be an holy convocation unto you: ye shall do no servile work therein: it shall be a statute for ever in all your dwellings throughout your generations.

Leviticus 23:15-21

OUR PRESENT STUDY INTRO-duces the middle feast of Israel's seven sacred observances. The first three feasts presented clearly their *primary association* with the nation Israel, their *personal application* for God's people at all times, and their *prophetic anticipation* of a glorious future. We have seen the logical progression of events in God's prophetic calendar, finding their fulfillment in the person and work of our Lord Jesus Christ. Here one sees the perfect harmony between the Old and the New Testaments.

Passover finds its fulfillment in the death of Christ "For even Christ our passover is sacrificed for us" (1 Corinthians 5:7). Calvary's cross works a new beginning for the sinner who puts his faith in the lamb of God who takes away sin (John 1:29). It is the vital point of contact between God and the believing sinner, establishing union between them. We have called this first feast the feast of *salvation*. The salvation of man appears first in God's calendar because this is His greatest concern. God's redemption is centered in Christ the Passover lamb.

The second feast, Unleavened Bread, began the day following Passover and is directly connected with it. In establishing this feast God is seeking to memorialize Israel's redemption from Egypt with its pagan, evil life. Leaven in the Bible always represents evil. It had to be removed from every dwelling of God's redeemed people. Holiness of life is a prime requisite for God's people everywhere. Christ the Passover lamb was without blemish. We cannot be perfectly sinless in this life as He was, but He is our perfect example. Holiness is an essential element for our communion with God. We have called this second feast the feast of *sanctification*.

The third feast, the Feast of Firstfruits, is closely associated with the first two both in time as well as in the truth they teach. During the days of unleavened bread, the day after the Sabbath, the people were to bring to the priest a sheaf of the first-ripe grain. The priest would present each sheaf to the Lord, thereby acknowledging thanksgiving to God who gave the bountiful harvest. This honored God and reminded the people that the entire harvest belonged to Him. God is the owner of the earth and its fruits; His people are His custodians, His caretakers, His stewards. The practical lesson for the believer in the third feast is *stewardship.*

But according to God's calendar there is a prophetic prospect for the believer. After our Lord was crucified He arose from the dead. At once we see how "the Old is in the New revealed." The apostle wrote, "But now is Christ risen from the dead, and become the firstfruits of them that slept" (1 Corinthians 15:20). "Christ the firstfruits, afterward they that are Christ's at his coming" (15:23). The risen Christ guarantees our resurrection. Paul testified before Agrippa "that Christ should suffer, and that he should be the first that should rise from the dead, and should show light unto the people, and the Gentiles" (Acts 26:23). The "people" in this text are Christ's own people, the Jews. And so, by reason of His resurrection, He assures a future resurrection for both believing Jews and Gentiles. In this the believer finds his security.

The middle feast of the seven holy convocations comes into view next. There are no less than four references where it is called "the feast of weeks" (Exodus 34:2; Deuteronomy 16:10,16; 2 Corinthians 8:13). The idea of weeks is suggested in Leviticus 23:15 where it states, "Seven sabbaths shall be completed." (Seven Sabbaths would mean seven weeks.) The most common designation for the fourth feast is Pentecost. Here we are introduced to something new.

"And ye shall count unto you from the morrow after the sabbath, from the day that ye brought the sheaf of the wave offering; seven sabbaths shall be complete: Even unto the morrow after the seventh sabbath shall ye number fifty days; and ye shall offer a new meat offering unto the LORD" (Leviticus 23:15-16).

69

Because of the widespread misunderstanding about the word *Pentecost,* there are some basic truths we need to know. The word itself is derived from the Greek word *pentekostos,* meaning fiftieth. Since the feast was celebrated on the fiftieth day after firstfruits, it is called the Feast of Pentecost.

At once the student of the Bible can see in God's prophetic calendar the chronological and orderly sequence of events. The type and anti-type are not left to our imagination or speculation. Luke penned the divinely-inspired meaning when he wrote, "And when the day of Pentecost was fully come . . ."(Acts 2:1), the word *fully* suggesting the fulfillment of the prophecy in God's prophetic calendar as He gave it in Leviticus 23. It was exactly fifty days after the resurrection of Christ that the Holy Spirit came. The events were coming to pass according to God's calendar, precisely on time. Passover had to precede Firstfruits, and Firstfruits had to precede Pentecost. Our Lord had to die before He could rise again, and He had to ascend to heaven glorified before the Holy Spirit could come. When Christ was here on earth, "The Holy Ghost was not yet given; because that Jesus was not yet glorified" (John 7:39). The coming of the Holy Spirit on the day of Pentecost marked a new entry on God's calendar, called "a new meat offering unto the LORD" (Leviticus 23:16).

What is this new entry, this new offering unto the Lord? We have seen already that Passover had its fulfillment in the death of Christ, and Firstfruits had its fulfillment in His resurrection from among the dead. According to God's calendar, Pentecost follows Firstfruits. Now the question is: Has there been a fulfillment of Pentecost, and if so, what is it? The type and anti-type are quite clear. Acts 2:1 is the fulfillment of the type in the fourth of the seven feasts, for on the fiftieth day after our Lord's resurrection the Holy Spirit came down from heaven. On that

70

day He inaugurated a new thing on the earth, called also "the firstfruits unto the Lord" (Leviticus 23:17).

The new thing is the church. When our Lord said, "I will build my church; and the gates of hell shall not prevail against it" (Matthew 16:18), the church was still future. It is obvious that the appearing of the Holy Spirit on the day of Pentecost was the fulfillment of the type of the presentation of the two wave loaves to the Lord in Leviticus 23:17.

This is a problem with some Christians, particularly those persons who fail to distinguish the difference between Israel and the church, or others who set the time of the church's birth at a later period in the book of Acts. However, there is really no excuse for this because of the plain teaching of the Bible. In our present study we have an excellent example of this. The time period for the church's beginning was set by God and fixed permanently in His calendar. That is one theme that stands out clearly in the seven feasts, particularly the Feast of Pentecost.

Consider first, *the foundation of the church.* The Lord Jesus Christ is both the founder and foundation of the church. He said, "I will build my church" (Matthew 16:18). The church is not built upon Peter as Romanism claims. A church that has Peter as its founder and foundation has little or nothing to offer lost sinners. Look carefully at our Lord's words to Peter: "And I say also unto thee, That thou art Peter, and upon this rock I will build my church; and the gates of hell shall not prevail against it" (Matthew 16:18). The Greek word for Peter is *petros,* meaning "a detached stone that might be easily moved," an accurate description of that vacillating apostle. The Greek word for rock is *petra,* "a strong rock that cannot be moved." To Israel, Jehovah was the rock (Deuteronomy 32:4,15,18,30-31). David said, "The LORD is my rock, and my fortress, and my deliverer" (2 Samuel 22:2). (See also Psalm 18:2,31,46.) Writing of Moses and Israel, Paul said, "They drank of that spiritual rock that followed them, and that rock was Christ" (1 Corinthians 10:1-4). Christ is both the founder and foundation of His church. "For other foundation can no man lay than that is laid, which is Jesus Christ" (1 Corinthians 3:11). We must turn to the Bible for the eternal and absolute truth.

Consider second, *the formation of the church*. One of the main features of the ritual of the Feast of Weeks was the presentation of the two loaves to the Lord (Leviticus 23:17). But why two loaves? The number of the loaves represents the two component parts of the church: believing Jews and believing Gentiles, both having been reconciled to God in one body through faith in the crucified and risen Son of God (Ephesians 2:13-18).

The Feast of Pentecost was a prophecy and a portrait of the church. The Pentecostal Feast, with its two loaves, shows us the loving heart of God in the great and gracious influence of the Holy Spirit, demonstrated on the day of Pentecost when three thousand souls were added to the church, which is Christ's body (Ephesians 1:22-23).

The Lord Jesus Christ is the bread of life to both Jews and Gentiles. Thus the evangelization of the whole world is the church's responsibility in the present Pentecostal dispensation. "For by one Spirit are we all baptized into one body, whether we be Jews or Gentiles, whether we be bond or free: and have been all made to drink into one Spirit" (1 Corinthians 12:13). In the old Jewish dispensation Pentecost was pointing to that day, fifty days after the resurrection of the Messiah, when Jew and Gentile would come together to worship Jehovah through Him.

Two striking features mark this present church age. The one is that there is a man in heaven, the God-man, the Lord Jesus

Christ, "who . . . when he had by himself purged our sins, sat down on the right hand of the Majesty on high" (Hebrews 1:3; see also 8:1; 10:12; 12:2). He is the Christian's representative before the Father, "seeing he ever liveth to make intercession for them" (Hebrews 7:25; 9:24). The Son of God who became our Passover and Firstfruits is presently our "merciful and faithful high priest" (Hebrews 2:17). The other amazing fact is that God the Holy Spirit has come to earth to continue the divine work of grace in and through every believer.

Consider first the Spirit's *incoming.* Immediately upon the sinner's faith in Christ, the Holy Spirit comes into his body. It is not possible that a person who has been born again does not have the Holy Spirit. A person without the Holy Spirit has never been saved. "Now if any man have not the Spirit of Christ, he is none of his" (Romans 8:9). One cannot belong to Christ and not have the Holy Spirit. It is "God who hath also given unto us his Holy Spirit" (1 Thessalonians 4:8). "And hereby we know that he abideth in us, by the Spirit which he hath given us" (1 John 3:24). (See also 1 Corinthians 3:16 and 6:19-20.)

Consider second, the Spirit's *indwelling.* Before our Lord gave Himself in death as our Passover and rose from death as the Firstfruits, He said to His disciples, "And I will pray the Father, and he shall give you another Comforter, that he may abide with you forever; Even the Spirit of truth, whom the world cannot receive, because it seeth him not, neither knoweth him: but ye know him; for he dwelleth with you, and shall be in you" (John 14:16-17). Before Pentecost the Holy Spirit did now dwell permanently *in* the believer. He came *upon* them and was *with* them anointing and enabling them to do God's work. The period of the judges illustrates this clearly. (See Judges 3:10; 6:34; 11:29; 13:25; 14:6,19; 15:14.) In John

73

14:16-17 our Lord was preparing the disciples for the transition from the "*with* you" experience to the "*in* you" experience. And He assured them that the Spirit's indwelling was to be permanent, "that he may abide with you forever" (John 14:16). In 1927 I received Jesus Christ as my Savior. On the day I was born of the Spirit (John 3:15), He took up His residence in my body. I have sinned during the years since, but the Holy Spirit has never departed from me.

Consider third, the Spirit's *infilling.* The one command in the Bible, addressed to all believers—to be filled with the Spirit—is in the Epistle to the Ephesians: "And be not drunk with wine, wherein is excess; but be filled with the Spirit" (Ephesians 5:18). Because of a widespread misunderstanding about being filled with the Spirit, a word of explanation is necessary as to the difference between being baptized with the Spirit and being filled with the Spirit. The Christian is commanded to be filled with the Spirit. However, there is no command in the Bible in which a child of God is told to be baptized with the Holy Spirit. Nor is there an exhortation in the Bible to believers to seek the baptism with the Spirit.

The baptism in (or with) the Spirit has been experienced by every Christian in the present church age. On the other hand, the baptizing work with the Spirit is never mentioned in past dispensations; it is something new in, and limited to, this present dispensation of the church. The Bible never mentions an Old Testament believer as having experienced the baptizing work with the Holy Spirit, or during the period of Christ's ministry on earth. After His resurrection and before His ascension to heaven, He said, "Ye shall be baptized with the Holy Ghost not many days hence" (Acts 1:5). It is quite clear from Scripture that, before our Lord's death (Passover) and resurrection (Firstfruits), the baptizing with the Holy Spirit was yet future.

This phase of the Spirit's ministry took place on the day of Pentecost, even as Peter testified (Acts 11:15-17).

So I repeat for emphasis that the baptism with the Spirit is the universal experience of every born-again person in this present church age. It is even as the apostle Paul wrote, "For by one Spirit are we all baptized into one body, whether we be Jews or Gentiles, whether we be bond or free; and have been all made to drink into one Spirit" (1 Corinthians 12:13). This is why you do not find anywhere in the New Testament a command or an exhortation to be baptized with the Holy Spirit. We never should confuse the baptism with the filling.

On the day of Pentecost the one true and living God, in the presence of the Holy Spirit, formed the church in an intimacy never before known. Every saved person is indwelt with the Holy Spirit (Romans 8:9), sealed with the Holy Spirit (Ephesians 2:13), and baptized with the Holy Spirit (1 Corinthians 12:13). It is a blessed and beautiful fact that the eternal God has become emotionally and organically identified with the human race. God does not need us, for He is self-sufficient. And yet He has sent both His Son and His Spirit to save us and bind us to Himself forever. Pentecost is a lesson in something new.

One further point of interest should not be neglected. The two loaves were to be baked with leaven. "They shall be baken with leaven" (Leviticus 23:17). We have already learned that leaven is a picture of sin, a principle of evil. Why then were these loaves to be baked with leaven?

The two loaves are a picture of the church, a composite of redeemed Jews and Gentiles. However, redeemed people are never free of the possibility of sin in this present life. There is sin in the church today. In every New Testament Epistle the Holy Spirit deals with the sin problem. After all, the church is

75

people: saved people, born again people, but not people who are perfectly sinless. "If we say that we have no sin, we deceive ourselves, and the truth is not in us" (1 John 1:8). Not until the church is caught up to heaven will the members be sinless. When our Lord appears to rapture His church, then "we shall be like him; for we shall see him as he is" (1 John 3:2), conformed to His image (Romans 8:29), "a glorious church, not having spot, or wrinkle, or any such thing" (Ephesians 5:27).

Some might say that the church with leaven in it is a sad and sorry mess. I will not agree to such a conclusion. I see faithful men and women every day who have committed themselves to serving the Lord Jesus Christ. Certainly, there was a Judas among our Lord's disciples, but there were His loyal servants also. Both kinds are obvious to the most casual observer. The visible churches on earth have sin in them if for no other reason than because you and I are in them. But God continues to get His work done in spite of us, because the Holy Spirit is here to "reprove the world of sin, and of righteousness, and of judgment" (John 16:7-8).

Peter was possibly the most vacillating of our Lord's redeemed followers, yet on that day of Pentecost the Holy Spirit used his preaching in the conversion of three thousand souls, all of whom were brought by the same Holy Spirit into one body, the church of the Lord Jesus Christ. And the same Spirit continues His work in and through the church today. More people are hearing the gospel than at any time in the history of the church. The door is open wide. The evangelization of the world is the church's privilege and responsibility in this Pentecostal dispensation. Let us praise God for the gift of the Holy Spirit and for all our spiritual blessings.

76

PART TWO

The Final Coming of Christ

Leviticus 23:23-44

*His Appearing Will
Be Personal*

*His Atonement Will
Be Perfected*

*His Authority Will
Be Preeminent*

5

The Feast of Trumpets

His Appearing Will Be Personal

Leviticus 23:23-25

The book of Leviticus communicates a word from God to contemporary believers. Leviticus speaks to so few today because so few believe that God can come to them through and yet beyond the words of another culture and time. But there is a timelessness about the reality of God's Word. For the Christian, Leviticus sketches sacrifice and atonement in finely detailed patterns which set the background for understanding Jesus' life and death.

ROY LEE HONEYCUTT, JR.

And the LORD spake unto Moses, saying, Speak
unto the children of Israel, saying, In the seventh
month, in the first day of the month, shall ye have
a sabbath, a memorial of blowing of trumpets, an
holy convocation. Ye shall do no servile work therein:
but ye shall offer an offering made by fire unto the
LORD.

Leviticus 23:23-25

VIEWING GOD'S PROPHETIC
calendar from where we are today, it is clear that the prophecies
in the first four feasts have been fulfilled. History bears out the
fact that they speak of a work God has already accomplished
for the salvation of both Jew and Gentile.

After the details were given regarding the Feast of Pentecost,
God added an important postscript. He said to His people
Israel, "And when ye reap the harvest of your land, thou shalt
not make clean riddance of the corners of thy field when thou
reapest, neither shalt thou gather any gleaning of thy harvest:
thou shalt leave them unto the poor, and to the stranger: I am
the LORD your God" (Leviticus 23:22). "The poor and the
stranger" are the Gentiles whom Paul called "aliens from the
commonwealth of Israel, and strangers from the covenants of
promise" (Ephesians 2:12). Following the death and resurrection of Christ (Passover and Firstfruits), and the coming of the
Holy Spirit (Pentecost), the church was formed of believing
Jews and Gentiles. All of this is history.

The next event on God's prophetic calendar is the Feast of
Trumpets. "And the LORD spake unto Moses, saying, Speak
unto the children of Israel, saying, In the seventh month, in

the first day of the month, shall ye have a sabbath, a memorial of blowing of trumpets, an holy convocation" (Leviticus 23:24). This is the first of the final three feasts, all looking ahead to a glorious future. In this present dispensation of the church we can see on God's calendar the coming events for both the church and Israel.

The fourth feast (Pentecost) was celebrated in the spring of the year. These last three feasts (Trumpets, Atonement, and Tabernacles) were in the fall of the year. From early in the third month till the first day of the seventh month, there was no holy convocation to be observed. Part of the third month and all of the fourth, fifth, and sixth months together constituted a waiting period. This period of time between the Feast of Pentecost and the Feast of Trumpets was the longest period of time between any of the other feasts.

Is there a lesson to be gleaned from the long interval between the Feast of Pentecost and the Feast of Trumpets? I believe there is a matter of special significance too obvious to pass by. The seven feasts, in their primary association, were enjoined upon the children of Israel. When reading Leviticus 23 this fact stands forth, even to the casual reader. "And the LORD spake unto Moses, saying, Speak unto the children of Israel . . ." (23:1-2,9-10,23-24,33-34). "And Moses declared unto the children of Israel the feasts of the LORD" (23:44). The Gentile nations had no part in those holy convocations.

But as we follow God's prophetic calendar we are presently in the dispensation of the church. The gospel must go to all the world, to every creature (Mark 16:15; Acts 1:8). Any Jew or Gentile can be saved through faith in the Lord Jesus Christ and thereby become a member of the church.

But God is not now dealing with Israel as a nation. What God is doing today during the interval between Pentecost and

Trumpets is not a part of Jewish prophecy nationally. The nation of Israel is in a holding pattern, in God's waiting room, waiting for the sound of the trumpet. There is a bright future for the nation of Israel. However, the waiting period has been a long one, the longest in the history of man. There has been no period in human history, as long as the present one, in which God has not intervened in behalf of the nation Israel. Two thousand years have come and gone and Israel continues to wait for the sound of the trumpet. Since their rejection of the Messiah, God has remained silent.

God has His reasons for this long interval between the Feast of Pentecost and the Feast of Trumpets. Prophetically there is nothing in the Bible telling us why God has stretched out this long interval, nor precisely how long it will be. But we do know that ours is the dispensation of grace, not one of judgment. Judgment is coming, to be sure, "But, beloved, be not ignorant of this one thing, that one day is with the Lord as a thousand years, and a thousand years as one day. The Lord is not slack concerning his promise, as some men count slackness; but is longsuffering to usward, not willing that any should perish, but that all should come to repentance" (2 Peter 3:8-9).

At the council of the apostles and elders in Jerusalem, speaking of the present church age, James reminded them "how God at the first did visit the Gentiles, to take out of them a people for his name" (Acts 15:14). But by no means was there an implication that there was no future for Israel. The holy convocation of trumpets in God's calendar looks forward to the next events in the prophetic program. James continued his testimony at the council with the following: "And to this agree the words of the prophets; as it is written, After this I will return, and will build again the tabernacle of David, which is fallen down; and I will build again the ruins thereof, and I will set it up" (Acts 15:15-16). In his reference to the prophets, James doubtless had in mind the prophecy of Amos who wrote: "In that day will I raise up the tabernacle of David that is fallen, and close up the breaches thereof; and I will raise up his ruins, and I will build it as in the days of old" (Amos 9:11). Micah likewise declared, "In the day that thy walls are to be built, in that day shall the decree be far removed" (Micah 7:11). The prophets were pointing ahead to an event which God had written into His calendar and which He called the Feast of Trumpets. It is inseparably linked with the second coming of Christ. In fact, our Lord's second coming is the main truth associated with this fifth feast.

The idea of trumpets originated with God. Today we have modern means of communication whereby an event taking place in any part of the world can be brought into our livingroom with sound and sight. Advanced technology has given to the world an audio and visual communication system enabling us to both see and hear what is taking place.

In ancient times God gave to Israel a communication system. He gave instructions to Moses for the making of the trumpet. The first mention of the trumpet in the Bible is connected with the giving of the Ten Commandments at Sinai (Exodus 19:13-20). The trumpet was used to assemble the people to work, worship, and warfare (Numbers 10:1-10). Through the communication system of trumpet sounds, God made a profound impression upon Israel. It was a vital link in the relationship between Him and His people. When the watchmen at their posts saw an enemy approaching, they blew trumpets to warn the people. When the hour for worship drew near, they sounded the call with trumpets. It was very important that the trumpeters be accurate in sounding every note, "For if the trumpet give an uncertain sound, who shall prepare himself to the battle?" (1 Corinthians 14:8).

The Israelites, however, did not obey God in spite of the fact that they received a clear and intelligent communication from Him. As a result, God refused to continue communicating with them. Between the Old and New Testaments there were four silent centuries during which there was no word from God. Then God sent His Son, whom they rejected and crucified. Today, during the church age, they are not in the program of God. Israel has been temporarily set aside while God works through the church. So it is not mere chance that, since Christ came to His own and His own rejected Him (John 1:11), the temple has been destroyed and the Jewish people have been scattered into many parts of the earth.

The many pogroms and persecutions against the children of Israel are not by chance or accident. God is sovereign and in control of His world and the people in it. The present rejection of Israel by God is a divinely-executed punitive and corrective measure. God had warned Israel that failure to obey Him would result in hardship for them. Moses wrote, "Because thou wouldest not obey the voice of the LORD thy God . . . the LORD shall scatter thee among all people, from the one end of the earth even unto the other" (Deuteronomy 28:62-64).

While God is punishing Israel for their willful disobedience, He will by no means permit their complete and final destruction. Israel's present rejection is a temporary one. Our God made reference to both Israel's present rejection and prospective restoration when He said, "O Jerusalem, Jerusalem, thou that killest the prophets, and stonest them which are sent unto thee, how often would I have gathered thy children together, even as a hen gathereth her chickens under her wings, and ye would not! Behold, your house is left unto you desolate. For I say unto you, Ye shall not see me henceforth, till ye shall say, Blessed is he that cometh in the name of the Lord" (Matthew 23:37-39). Their rejection is limited "till" Messiah comes again and they shall say, "Blessed is he that cometh." That word *till* is a time word which places a definite limitation on how long the nation will remain scattered. There are those who believe and teach that there is no political or spiritual future for Israel, but they are wrong.

The apostle Paul, in his Epistle to the Romans, followed up our Lord's teaching on Israel's present rejection and prospective restoration when he wrote, "For I would not, brethren, that ye should be ignorant of this mystery, lest ye should be wise in your own conceits, that blindness in part is happened to Israel until the fulness of the Gentiles be come in" (Romans 11:25). Here Paul uses the time word *until*. The present blindness is only "in part," that is, not all Jews are cut off from the possibility of being saved during the present period of God's rejection of the nation. We saw in the Feast of Pentecost how that individual Jews as well as individual Gentiles have the same privilege and possibility of being saved during the church age. Nor is the blindness permanent. It is only "until" the times of the Gentiles run their course. As Luke stated it, "And they shall fall by the edge of the sword, and shall be led away captive into all nations: and Jerusalem shall be trodden down of the Gentiles, until the times of the Gentiles be fulfilled" (Luke 21:24).

And then Paul added, "And so all Israel shall be saved: as it is written, There shall come out of Sion the Deliverer, and shall turn away ungodliness from Jacob: For this is my covenant unto them, when I shall take away their sins" (Romans 11:26-27). Many who have read this passage found it difficult to understand. In using the words *all Israel* did Paul mean that every Jew would be saved? When would this salvation occur? What are the requirements for their salvation? What did Paul mean by the word *saved?*

When Paul said, "All Israel shall be saved," he did not mean that *every* Jew living when Christ returns to earth after the tribulation will be regenerated or born again. The word *saved* sometimes means "delivered" and is so used in both Testaments. When the Lord delivered Israel from the bondage of Egypt, "Moses said unto the people, Fear ye not, stand still, and see the salvation of the LORD" (Exodus 14:13). After the miraculous crossing of the Red Sea we read, "Thus the LORD saved Israel that day out of the hand of the Egyptians" (Exodus 14:30). Both the noun *salvation* and the verb *saved* are used in the sense of deliverance. When Peter walked on the water and began to sink, he cried, "Lord, save me" (Matthew 14:30). Then, he was asking the Lord to deliver him, to rescue him from drowning. It is that kind of deliverance Paul had in mind when he said, "All Israel shall be saved." Our Lord predicted that salvation in His Olivet discourse when He said, "But he that shall endure unto the end, the same shall be saved" (Matthew 24:13). All Jews who survive to the end of the great tribulation will experience a deliverance. Paul was not saying that all Jews who ever lived will be saved.

When will this deliverance occur? It will occur at the end of the tribulation, "As it is written, There shall come out of Sion the Deliverer" (Romans 11:26). The deliverer, of course, is the Lord Jesus Christ when He comes to earth the second time. Many Jews will perish during the judgments of the great tribulation (Jeremiah 30–31), but a surviving remnant will be saved.

What are the requirements for the salvation of the remnant? They will accept the deliverer as their Messiah and redeemer (Isaiah 53:4-6; Zechariah 12:10), and He "shall turn away ungodliness from Jacob" and "shall take away their sins" (Romans 11:26-27). For that remnant in Israel the deliverance will be both physical and spiritual as well as political. Israel's salvation will be the fulfillment of God's promise which He gave to His prophets (Isaiah 27:9; 59:20-21; Jeremiah 31:31-35). God Himself will accomplish this as the result of the unconditional covenant He made, a covenant based upon sovereign grace alone.

The chronological harmony of the feasts becomes clearer. When the church age (Pentecost) comes to its end, the Feast of Trumpets will begin. According to God's prophetic calendar, the next event that will link Pentecost to Trumpets is the second coming of the Lord Jesus Christ. His coming will be in two phases: (1) the pre-tribulation appearing in the air at which time He will remove His church from the earth; (2) His post-tribulation appearing on the earth when Israel will be re-gathered, restored permanently to the land, and reborn spiritually.

The next trumpet sound will terminate the present dispensation with the rapture of the church. "For the Lord himself shall descend from heaven with a shout, with the voice of the archangel, and with the trump of God: and the dead in Christ shall rise first: Then we which are alive and remain shall be caught up together with them in the clouds, to meet the Lord in the air: and so shall we ever be with the Lord" (1 Thessalonians 4:16-17). The first trumpet sound from heaven will signal Christ's special relationship with His church. It is called "the last trump" (1 Corinthians 15:51-52), meaning the last trumpet sound of this present dispensation of the church. The church's battle against the gates of hell will cease, and all the redeemed in Christ will be with Him forever.

But what is Israel's future? When our Lord predicted the

tribulation to befall the nation, He followed it with the prophecy: "Immediately after the tribulation of those days shall the sun be darkened, and the moon shall not give her light, and the stars shall fall from heaven, and the powers of heaven shall be shaken: And then shall all the tribes of the earth mourn, and they shall see the Son of man coming in the clouds of heaven with power and great glory. And he shall send his angels with a great sound of a trumpet, and they shall gather his elect from the four winds, from one end of heaven to the other" (Matthew 24:29-31). In that day of Israel's awakening, the Jewish remnant of the last days will hear the trumpet sound and respond to it. God will not remain silent forever. His scattered people will be regathered.

Our Lord's prophecy in Matthew 24:31 is no new thing to the Jew who has read his Old Testament. The prophet Isaiah wrote, "And it shall come to pass in that day, that the LORD shall beat off from the channel of the river unto the stream of Egypt, and ye shall be gathered one by one, O ye children of Israel. And it shall come to pass in that day, that the great trumpet shall be blown, and they shall come which were ready to perish in the land of Assyria, and the outcasts in the land of Egypt, and shall worship the LORD in the holy mount at Jerusalem" (Isaiah 27:12-13).

The prophet Joel wrote of "that day" when God will gather His people together at the sound of the trumpet:

> Blow the trumpet in Zion, sanctify a fast, call a solemn assembly: Gather the people, sanctify the congregation, assemble the elders, gather the children, and those that suck the breasts: let the bridegroom go forth of his chamber, and the bride out of her closet. Let the priests, the ministers of the LORD, weep between the porch and

89

the altar, and let them say, Spare thy people, O LORD, and give not thine heritage to reproach, that the heathen should rule over them: wherefore should they say among the people, Where is their God? Then will the LORD be jealous for his land, and pity his people. Yea, the LORD will answer and say unto his people, Behold, I will send you corn, and wine, and oil, and ye shall be satisfied therewith: and I will no more make you a reproach among the heathen: But I will remove far off from you the northern army, and will drive him into a land barren and desolate, with his face toward the east sea, and his hinder part toward the utmost sea, and his stink shall come up, and his ill savour shall come up, because he hath done great things. Fear not, O land; be glad and rejoice: for the LORD will do great things (Joel 2:15-21).

The full and final answer to the Feast of Trumpets may not be far removed from the present. What a glorious day for that nation, who have been in the slumber of spiritual death, when they behold their Messiah! They will, with genuine repentance and remorse, receive Him to rule over them.

I am sure that the great heart of God, who knows precisely when He will send forth the sound of the trumpet, first to gather His church to Himself and then to gather His beloved Israel to their land, awaits the completion of His redeeming work through His Son the Lord Jesus Christ. What a day when the final triumph will be heralded and the Feast of Trumpets will have come! This will begin the most joyous of all the seasons of the year and of all the holy convocations. Once again we have seen in God's calendar its prophetic implications.

I feel constrained to appeal to those persons who read these pages but who have not received the Lord Jesus Christ as your personal Savior. Between the trumpet sounds that will first rapture the church and then regather Israel, there are seven trumpets. They are recorded in detail in Revelation 8–9. They will announce a sequence of terrible judgments to be poured out on all persons who have rejected Jesus Christ. Time is running out for all such persons. "Behold, now is the accepted time; behold, now is the day of salvation" (2 Corinthians 6:2). "Believe on the Lord Jesus Christ, and thou shalt be saved, and thy house" (Acts 16:31).

6

The Feast of Atonement

His Atonement Will Be Perfected

Leviticus 23:26-32

Leviticus was penned to provide precise guidelines for sacrifice, worship, and service primarily for an elect nation but also for Gentiles who would trust and submit to Israel's God. Leviticus clearly sets forth and institutionalizes the system of substitutionary blood sacrifice. Regardless of how one may argue, God has established the principles of sacrifice. Not to accept His specific revelation concerning sacrifice will do irreparable harm to the soul.

LOUIS GOLDBERG

And the LORD spake unto Moses, saying, Also on the tenth day of this seventh month there shall be a day of atonement: it shall be an holy convocation unto you; and ye shall afflict your souls, and offer an offering made by fire unto the LORD. And ye shall do no work in that same day: for it is a day of atonement, to make an atonement for you before the LORD your God. For whatsoever soul it be that shall not be afflicted in that same day, he shall be cut off from among his people. And whatsoever soul it be that doeth work in that same day, the same soul will I destroy from among his people. Ye shall do no manner of work: it shall be a statute for ever throughout your generations in all your dwellings. It shall be unto you a sabbath of rest, and ye shall afflict your souls: in the ninth day of the month at even, from even unto even, shall ye celebrate your sabbath.

Leviticus 23:26-32

THE LAST THREE FEASTS IN God's prophetic calendar, Trumpets, Atonement, and Tabernacles, all look into the future from our present position in the church age. At the sound of the first trumpet, the church will be caught up to be with the Lord (1 Corinthians 15:52; 1 Thessalonians 4:16). The next trumpet sound after the rapture of the church will be the voice of God calling Jews back to their own land of Palestine. "Immediately after the tribulation . . . he shall send his angels with a great sound of a trumpet, and they shall gather together his elect from the four winds, from one end of heaven to the other" (Matthew 24:29-31). In that day no man or nation will be able to prevent the Jewish people from coming into their rightful place and possession. God's unconditional covenant with Abraham, which He confirmed later with Isaac and Jacob, will be finalized.

But Israel's greatest need is a spiritual one. Possessing the land and having protection from their enemies cannot solve the nation's biggest problem. Before the nation can enjoy lasting peace and protection, repentance and cleansing from sin are imperative. Suddenly awakened to a sense of their national sin, their sad lament will be, "The harvest is past, the summer is ended, and we are not saved" (Jeremiah 8:20). An awareness of the nation's unfaithfulness and rejection of their Messiah demands that they deal with the sin question. The idea of cleansing is the main lesson in the Feast of Atonement. This holy convocation is called "a day of atonement" (Leviticus 23:27).

The word *atonement* is an Old Testament term appearing no less than forty-eight times in the book of Leviticus. It appears once only in the King James translation of the New Testament: "And not only so, but we also joy in God through our Lord Jesus Christ, by whom we have now received the atonement" (Romans 5:11). But the marginal reference, along with later translations, reads "reconciliation." However, there is little difference between the words *atonement* and *reconciliation*. When a sinner becomes reconciled to God, there is "at-one-ment," the two being brought together in harmony.

This harmony with God, this peace with God, has been made possible only through the sacrificial death and shedding of the blood of the Lord Jesus Christ. "When we were enemies, we were reconciled to God by the death of his Son" (Romans 5:10). "And you, that were sometimes alienated and enemies in your mind by wicked works, yet now hath he reconciled in the body of his flesh through death" (Colossians 1:21-22). The claims of the holy God upon the sinner must be met by blood, for "without shedding of blood is no remission" (Hebrews

9:22). The sinner who has been cleansed by Christ's blood has been reconciled to God, and therefore is "at-one-ment" with God. Sin can only be atoned for by blood.

The great Day of Atonement for Israel in the past was possibly the most important and significant in the whole Mosaic system. When referring to the Day of Atonement the rabbis used the one simple word *Yama,* meaning *"The* Day." On that one day sin was dealt with more fully and adequately than on any other occasion or in any other ceremony. For the children of Israel the Day of Atonement was the greatest event of the entire year. On that day forgiveness and cleansing from sin were not merely for individuals, but for all the sins of the whole nation. Wherever Jews honored the traditions of the Mosaic system, Yom Kippur, or the Day of Atonement, was observed. It was the most solemn of all Jewish holy days, *the* day when everyone sought forgiveness for all sins, intentional or unintentional.

In order for the student of the Bible to understand more clearly the meaning and importance of the Day of Atonement, Leviticus 16 must be examined carefully. This chapter is the heart of the sacrificial system for Israel. In this one chapter alone the word *atonement* appears fifteen times. It should be understood clearly that Leviticus 16, in its primary interpretation, relates to the nation of Israel. However, one will find some spiritual applications for all believers in Christ because the holy convocation on the annual Day of Atonement is a clear illustration of Christ's work for sin and all sinners. All of this shows up clearly in this sixteenth chapter which is the very heart and center of the book of Leviticus.

In Leviticus 16 frequent mention is made of *blood,* the word itself appearing not less than nine times. The two terms, *blood* and *atonement,* are never disassociated in the Mosaic system. "For the life of the flesh is in the *blood:* and I have given it to you upon the altar to make an *atonement* for your souls: for it is the *blood* that maketh an *atonement* for the soul" (Leviticus 17:11). Here we see another clear illustration of Christ's work for sinners. The writer to the Hebrews said, "And almost all things are by the law purged with blood; and without shedding of blood is no remission" (Hebrews 9:22). Frequently the word *blood* in the New Testament is associated with the death of Christ on the cross, sometimes called "the blood of the New Testament" (Matthew 26:28; Mark 14:24; Luke 22:20; 1 Corinthians 11:25; Hebrews 9:14-15). The New is in the Old concealed; the Old is in the New revealed. Someone expressed it as follows: The New is in the Old contained; the Old is by the New explained.

These seven religious festivals were especially ordained of God. Moreover, they were designed to impress upon the people the fact of God's holiness and how they could approach God. It was necessary therefore that the sins of the people be dealt with. The national corruption which crept into Israel brought forth from God's inspired prophet the following indictment: "Your iniquities have separated between you and your God, and your sins have hid his face from you, that he will not hear" (Isaiah 59:2). It was necessary therefore that all sins be atoned for, and the atonement necessitated a blood sacrifice. Here in Leviticus 16 we learn how sin is dealt with comprehensively, completely, and conditionally. At once we can see why the Day of Atonement was the most significant in the entire Mosaic system.

THE PRIEST

Looking at Leviticus 16 historically, it unfolds an accurate record of what actually took place in Israel on the great Day of Atonement. It was a unique day in Israel because it was the one day in the year when the holiness of God was vindicated and atonement provided for the sins of the people. The holiness of God and the sinfulness of man are the main subjects.

The chapter commences with reference to the incident recorded in chapter 10, namely, the death of Nadab and Abihu, the two oldest sons of Aaron. God struck those two young men dead in the court of the tabernacle. Earlier I suggested some possible reasons why this severe judgment from God came upon them. The priest in Israel was God's representative man to the people, therefore it was essential that he qualify at all times for his sacred ministry. On the Day of Atonement the priest must bring a sacrifice to atone for his own sins.

Special instructions were given by God for the priest, warning him that he should not come into the holy place to appear before God at all times (16:2). When he did appear on the Day of Atonement once each year, he needed to prepare himself for the sacred services before he could enter the holy of holies. That preparation necessitated the sacrifice of a young bullock. "And Aaron shall offer his bullock of the sin offering, which is for himself, and make an atonement for himself, and for his house" (16:6). His personal preparation included the washing of his body before he put on the holy garments (16:4). After bathing, he put on the garments, killed the bullock (16:11), entered the holy of holies "within the veil," and sprinkled the blood seven times before the mercy seat (16:14). Before he could represent the people of Israel before God, he first had to be acceptable to God, cleansed and forgiven of his own sins.

Louis Goldberg suggests that the presentation of the blood of the bull by the high priest represented, by identification, a new life for the priest. The blood represented forgiveness and the gift of a new life, which God alone was able to provide.

Hopefully, the high priest would come to know experientially the real meaning of the exchange-of-life principle and would truly know the Lord.

By contrast, our great high priest, the mediator of the new covenant, needed no sacrifice for Himself before He could represent us. He was the one man "who did no sin" (1 Peter 2:22) because "in him is no sin" (1 John 3:5). Unlike Israel's high priest, that nation's Messiah did not have to offer sacrifices for Himself before appearing in the presence of God in our behalf. The shed blood of bulls and goats was offered as a sacrifice for Israel's sinning priests (Hebrews 9:7). "But Christ being come a high priest of good things to come, by a greater and more perfect tabernacle, not made with hands, that is to say, not of this building; Neither by the blood of goats and calves, but by his own blood he entered in once into the holy place, having obtained eternal redemption for us" (Hebrews 9:11-12).

The work of Israel's high priest is contrasted further with that of our great high priest of whom the New Testament writer said, "Such an high priest became us, who is holy, harmless, undefiled, separate from sinners . . . ; Who needeth not daily, as those high priests, to offer up sacrifice, first for his own sins, and then for the people's" (Hebrews 7:26-27). The Day of Atonement was for Israel's high priest an awesome experience.

THE PEOPLE

After Aaron the priest had offered a sacrifice for himself and his family, special attention must be given to the sins of the people. The Day of Atonement for the people of Israel is described for us in several verses in Leviticus 16. Two goats were selected to be used in the ritual on behalf of the congregation of Israel. One would be slain as the sin offering for the people; the other would be the scapegoat.

> And he shall take of the congregation of the children of Israel two kids of the goats for a sin offering. . . . And he shall take the two goats, and present them before the LORD at the door of the tabernacle of the congregation. And Aaron shall cast lots upon the two goats; one for the LORD, and the other lot for the scapegoat. And Aaron shall bring the goat upon which the LORD's lot fell, and offer him for a sin offering. But the goat, on which the lot fell to be the scapegoat, shall be presented alive before the LORD, to make an atonement with him, and to let him go for a scapegoat into the wilderness (Leviticus 16:5, 7-10). Then shall he kill the goat of the sin offering, that is for the people (16:15). And Aaron shall lay both his hands upon the head of the live goat, and confess over him all the iniquities of the children of Israel, and all their transgressions in all their sins, putting them upon the head of the goat, and shall send him away by the hand of a fit man into the wilderness: And the goat shall bear upon him all their iniquities unto a land not inhabited: and he shall let go the goat in the wilderness (16:21-22).

A vivid picture of atonement is presented in the account of the two goats. One goat was designated "for the LORD, and the other for the scapegoat" (16:8). The goat for the Lord was slain and presented for "a sin offering" (16:9). Verse 15 makes the point that the blood of the slain goat was presented to the Lord "for the people." The sacrifice of the slain goat and sprinkling of its blood signified the means of reconciliation with God. It was important that the sins of the people be dealt with and this necessitated the blood sacrifice. However, the goat that was slain did not indicate the full meaning of the atonement. While' the atonement was the aim and purpose of the sin offering, it did never take away sin.

In the Old Testament the Hebrew word *kapar* means "to cover or conceal." Atonement would denote covering a person's sin, thereby making it possible for him to approach God. Since sin alienates man from God, the atoning sacrifice on the Day of Atonement was God's solution to this basic problem. The sacrificial animal was a "sin offering for the people." On the Day of Atonement, everyone sought forgiveness for all sins, intentional or unintentional; the blood sacrifice gave assurance that their sins were covered.

But the ceremony was incomplete until the high priest returned to the second goat who remained alive. "And Aaron shall lay both his hands upon the head of the live goat, and confess over him all the iniquities of the children of Israel, and all their transgressions in all their sins, putting them upon the head of the goat, and shall send him away by the hand of a fit man into the wilderness: And the goat shall bear upon him all their iniquities unto a land not inhabited: and he shall let go the goat into the wilderness" (16:21–22). As the Israelite watched his sins being carried away into the wilderness, he knew that God not only forgave his sins, but removed them from him. The atonement included not only the forgiveness of sins but the removal of them. David knew the full meaning of atonement when he wrote, "As far as the east is from the west, so far hath he removed our transgressions from us" (Psalm 103:12). One can imagine the excitement for the Israelite when he saw his sins being carried away into the wilderness, never to be charged against him again.

Finally, the people had enjoined upon them a solemn responsibility. It came in the form of a command: "Ye shall afflict your souls. . . . And ye shall do no work in that same day" (23:27-32). Their response to this command did in no way contribute to the forgiveness of their sins. They did nothing toward their atonement; the priest did it all. Salvation is never by works in any dispensation. Abstaining from work and showing sorrow for their sins on the Day of Atonement did not contribute a thing toward their forgiveness. They interrupted their busy lives for one day in humiliation of soul to accept by faith the forgiveness God provided for them.

The question has been asked, "If we are following a logical sequence or pattern of any kind, why wasn't the Day of Atonement placed first in the order of the convocation? It seems reasonable that the first thing that should happen in the plan of redemption is that sin should be taken care of completely." I am not sure that I have a satisfactory answer to this question. However, I will offer a suggestion. The Passover lamb whose blood was shed and applied had its beginning in Egypt and was a shield to protect the Israelites from the judgment of death. The Day of Atonement was never kept in Egypt. It awaited the construction of the tabernacle. The blood of the Passover lamb protected the Israelite from the judgment that falls upon unbelievers. The blood of atonement provided cleansing from those sins committed by God's children after they had been redeemed from Egypt.

There is a lesson in this for all Christians. We sin in thought, word, and action. Even as we grow in Christlikeness, we become aware of the problem of sin in our lives. So there is the need for us to draw daily from the power of Christ's atonement to overcome "the sin which doth so easily beset us" (Hebrews 12:1). God does not redeem us because we are holy, "But God commendeth his love toward us, in that, while we were yet sinners, Christ died for us" (Romans 5:8). He saved us as sinners that He might make us holy.

God Himself is holy. Our wonderful high priest, the Lord Jesus Christ, is holy. The Spirit who indwells us is holy. The Scriptures He inspired are holy. Paul describes our calling as "an holy calling" (2 Timothy 1:9). So then, the call to practical holiness is one we must anticipate after we become God's children. "But if we walk in the light as he is in the light, we have fellowship one with another, and the blood of Jesus Christ his Son cleanseth [i.e., keeps on cleansing] us from all sin" (1 John 1:7). The ritual on the Day of Atonement reached its climax when contrition and confession of sin occurred.

THE PROPHECY

We must give serious thought to the prophetic anticipation taught in the ceremony associated with the Day of Atonement. The seven Holy Convocations were arranged originally for the nation Israel, but God never intended that the nation should go through a mere religious ritual of formality. God intended that the people would experience the salvation of their souls and the forgiveness of sins. Every Israelite needed to know that his standing before the Lord was of primary importance, so when the great Day of Atonement approached, each individual was challenged to examine himself for personal impurities. The basic lesson was the need for contrition, confession, and forgiveness. So the tenth day of the seventh month became the most important day of the year in their religious calendar—a day of fasting, prayer, and deep searching of soul. Keep in mind the fact that, every year on that great Day of Atonement, the blood sacrifice had to be offered.

104

Amid the moving currents of change within the nation Israel, the greatest tragedy is the continuing attempt to have a Day of Atonement without the blood sacrifice of a sin offering. Our dear Jewish friends appear to be totally unmindful of God's clear statement: "For the life of the flesh is in the blood: and I have given it to you upon the altar to make an atonement for your souls: for it is the blood that maketh an atonement for the soul" (Leviticus 17:11). Every Sabbath, Old Testament Scriptures are read to Jews when they gather in their synagogues. Still, they go through the formalities without the blood sacrifice, the vital focus-point of the Day of Atonement, the very heart of the sacrificial system. Just as blood gives life to the body, so the blood of the animal sacrifice (representing its life) was accepted by God as atonement in providing new life. The life of the substitute interposed between God and the sinner. This is the real meaning of atonement.

Liberalism in Judaism, like liberalism in Protestant denominations, questions whether blood is necessary for salvation and the forgiveness of sins. The question is not debatable, nor will I attempt to discuss the question whether God could have provided redemption and forgiveness in some other way without blood. Let the sincere Jew take God at His word as it is in Leviticus 17:11, and the sincere Gentile do the same as it is stated in Hebrews 9:22, and the case is settled and closed forever. In the levitical system a blood sacrifice was God's appointed method of atoning for sin. God's plan for reconciling the sinner to Himself requires that each of us identify with the death of a substitute, the only means of reconciliation. We know that the Lord Jesus Christ is that substitute. For two thousand years Israel has rejected the Messiah, the lamb of God, who "taketh away the sin of the world" (John 1:29). If

God is to save the Jew, it must be in a way which is in harmony with His holiness, His hatred for sin, and His perfect way of doing it.

But what hope is there for the Jewish nation? The prophecy in God's calendar answers that question with unmistakable clarity. There is yet a future Day of Atonement when the nation will know confession, cleansing, and forgiveness. Go back and read carefully, slowly, and meditatively the entire ceremony involving the priest, the place where the sacrifice was offered to the Lord and the people. In that ceremony can be seen a beautiful picture of the future cleansing of Israel. In the preceding study of the Feast of Trumpets, we learned that in a future day God will sound a trumpet to gather Israel back to the land. The Old Testament prophets (Isaiah 27:12-13; Joel 2:15-21) wrote of that bright prospect for God's beloved Israel. Now what follows chronologically the Feast of Trumpets? Of course, the Day of Atonement.

The prophet Jeremiah speaks of that long-awaited day. "In those days, and in that time, saith the LORD, the iniquity of Israel shall be sought for, and there shall be none; and the sins of Judah, and they shall not be found: for I will pardon them whom I reserve" (Jeremiah 50:20). There is both a future gathering and a future glory for Israel. This will all come to pass after the Feast of Trumpets, after "he shall send his angels with a great sound of a trumpet, and they shall gather together his elect from the four winds, from one end of heaven to the other" (Matthew 24:31). The Day of Atonement appears after the second coming of our Lord and before His kingly reign on earth.

The prophet Zechariah wrote of that future Day of Atonement: "And it shall come to pass in that day, that I will seek to destroy all the nations that come against Jerusalem. And I will pour upon the house of David, and upon the inhabitants of Jerusalem, the [S]pirit of grace and of supplications: and they shall look upon me whom they have pierced, and they shall mourn for him, as one mourneth for his only son, and shall be in bitterness for him, as one that is in bitterness for his firstborn. In that day shall there be a great mourning in Jerusalem" (Zechariah 12:9-11). I have spelled the word *Spirit* in verse 10 with a capital "S" because Israel's deliverance from sin will be accomplished by the Holy Spirit, leading the Israelites to repentant faith in Jesus Christ as their Messiah. The "mourning" in verses 10 and 11 corresponds to the "affliction of soul" in Leviticus 16:29-31 and 23:27-32. Genuine repentance and sorrow for sin is always the result of the work of the Holy Spirit. In that day He will minister graciously to Israel in their unbelief and will lead them to contrition and confession of sin. The weeping and mourning of Israel over their sin of rejecting the Messiah is likened to the weeping on the day when the godly King Josiah was slain by Pharaoh Neco II, at Hadad Rimmon. (See 2 Chronicles 35:20-27.)

"In that day there shall be a fountain opened to the house of David and to the inhabitants of Jerusalem for sin and for uncleanness" (Zechariah 13:1). "That day" is synonymous with "the day of the LORD" in 14:1. The phrase "on that day" occurs no less than sixteen times in the three concluding chapters (12:3,4,6,8,9,11; 13:1,2,4; 14:4,6,8,9,13,20,21). The day our Lord died on the cross, the fountain was opened immediately for any and all to receive cleansing from sin, and for Israel *potentially, prophetically,* and *experientially.* The prophetic fulfillment for Israel of the great Day of Atonement will be the nation's greatest and most glorious day. All forms of idolatry and every evil spirit will be banished from the land. Jeremiah (31:31-37) and Ezekiel (36:25-32) both depict details related to the future national repentance and sorrow of Israel over the Messiah "whom they have pierced." On that day of Israel's national atonement, the iniquity of the land shall be removed "in one day" (Zechariah 3:9).

The fountain that shall be opened to the inhabitants of Jerusalem for sin and for uncleanness is most certainly the blood of the Messiah "whom they have pierced" (Zechariah 12:10). The terms *pierced* in 12:10 and *fountain* in 13:1 are no doubt linked together. It has been objected by some scholars that the "fountain" could not be the blood of Christ shed at Calvary nineteen centuries ago because the national cleansing of Israel is yet future. I have no problem with the time element between the two events. The fountain for Israel's future cleansing remains open today for sinners to experience cleansing and forgiveness of sins as they receive the Lord Jesus Christ. People continue to be saved through faith in His blood (Romans 5:9) nineteen hundred years removed from Christ's death. That fountain remains open today.

There is a bright future for Israel. People should be careful of criticizing God's nation Israel, and governments should move slowly in their condemnation of this special group. The nations that oppose Israel are opposing themselves. The unconditional promises God made to Abram, when He first called him out from a pagan world, have been incorporated into the formal Abrahamic Covenant. When the nation repents and mourns over their Messiah—a mourning that will be individual, personal, and national—the breach will be healed finally and forever.

7

The Feast of Tabernacles

His Authority Will Be Preeminent

Leviticus 23:33-44

The Feasts of Jehovah contain in typical language, a record of God's dealings with man in grace, from the death of Christ to His millennial kingdom, and to the eternal glory and rest which lie beyond it. It is also a prophecy, a foreshadowing of great events of the future, part of which have since been fulfilled, and part of which are yet to be.

JOHN RITCHIE

7

The Feast of Tabernacles

His Authority Will Be Preeminent

Leviticus 23:33-44

And the LORD spake unto Moses, saying, The fifteenth day of this seventh month shall be the feast
of tabernacles for seven days unto the LORD. On
the first day shall be an holy convocation: ye shall
do no servile work therein. Seven days ye shall offer
an offering made by fire unto the LORD: on the
eighth day shall be an holy convocation unto you;
and ye shall offer an offering made by fire unto the
LORD: it is a solemn assembly; and ye shall do no
servile work therein. These are the feasts of the LORD,
a burnt offering, and a meat offering, a sacrifice, and
drink offerings, everything upon his day: Beside the
sabbaths of the LORD, and beside your gifts, and
beside all your vows, and beside all your freewill
offerings, which ye give unto the LORD. Also in the
fifteenth day of the seventh month, when ye have
gathered in the fruit of the land, ye shall keep a feast
unto the LORD seven days: on the first day shall be
a sabbath, and on the eighth day shall be a sabbath.
And ye shall take you on the first day the boughs
of goodly trees, branches of palm trees, and the
boughs of thick trees and willows of the brook; and
ye shall rejoice before the LORD your God seven
days. And ye shall keep it a feast unto the LORD
seven days in the year. It shall be a statute for ever
in your generations: ye shall celebrate it in the
seventh month. Ye shall dwell in booths seven days:
all that are Israelites born shall dwell in booths: That
your generations may know that I made the children
of Israel to dwell in booths, when I brought them

out of the land of Egypt: I am the LORD your God.
And Moses declared unto the children of Israel the
feasts of the LORD.

Leviticus 23:33-44

IN AMERICA THE FOURTH
Thursday in November is marked on every calendar as
Thanksgiving Day. It had its origin early in our nation's history
when the settlers came together to offer thanks to God after
the final ingathering of the crops in the fall of the year. The
important feature of this celebration was the time spent in
reflecting upon the mercy and blessing of the Lord for His
bountiful provision. Thanksgiving Day has always been a time
of feasting and rejoicing.

The Feast of Tabernacles compares in some ways to our
annual Thanksgiving Day. It was the seventh and final feast,
completing the sacred cycle of the Lord's appointed times. It
was a fitting conclusion to the entire series of seven. Verse 36
calls it "a solemn assembly," translated by some scholars as
"the closing assembly." In its prophetic foreview and chronological arrangement in God's calendar, it brought to completion
God's clear purposes and plans in redemption for both the
church and Israel. Man's day will have run its course and God's
redeemed ones will be gathered to Himself. This feast was to
be kept after all the harvest had been reaped. It is the Feast
of Ingathering, the summation of events in God's calendar.

This final feast commenced on the fifteenth day of the
seventh month and continued for seven days (23:34,39). God

had said, "Thou shalt observe the feast of tabernacles seven days, after thou hast gathered in thy corn and thy wine" (Deuteronomy 16:13). When our Lord was here on earth He said, "Verily, verily, I say unto you, Except a corn of wheat fall into the ground and die, it abideth alone: but if it die, it bringeth forth much fruit" (John 12:24). Christ was that corn (grain) of wheat. He did die and rise again from death and the grave. In the end of God's dealings with man, Christ will have gathered His own to Himself. The harvest will be completed, even to the gathering of His enemies for judgment. Both the corn and the wine will be brought before Him. The vintage of the earth, the treading of the winepress of divine wrath, may refer to the gathering of the enemies of God for judgment.

Just as this feast marked the final gathering of "the fruit of the land" (23:39), so there will be a final gathering of all mankind, both the "wheat" and the "tares," which are the children of Christ's kingdom and the children of the wicked one (Matthew 13:24-30,36-43). (See Revelation 14:18-19 and 19:15.) These are the two divisions of the harvest.

This final convocation has been called the Feast of Booths, because the people left their dwellings to camp out in tent-like huts for seven days. "Ye shall dwell in booths seven days; all that are Israelites born shall dwell in booths" (Leviticus 23:42). The booths were to be made of boughs of fruit trees, palm branches, leafy tree limbs, and willow branches (23:40). Imagine, if you can, those Jews coming out from their houses every year to live one week in a frail shelter made from the branches of trees.

But why did God single out one nation from all the nations of the earth, and deal with them in this way? God had His reasons, we are sure.

113

A TIME TO REMEMBER

"And Moses commanded them, saying, At the end of every seven years, in the solemnity of the year of release, in the feast of tabernacles, When all Israel is come to appear before the LORD thy God in the place which he shall choose, thou shalt read this law before all Israel in their hearing. Gather the people together, men, and women, and children, and thy stranger that is within thy gates, that they may hear, and that they may learn, and fear the LORD your God, and observe to do all the words of this law: And that their children, which have not known any thing, may hear, and learn to fear the LORD your God, as long as ye live in the land whither ye go over Jordan to possess it" (Deuteronomy 31:10-13). Those booths, constructed with the products and fruits of the land, were a reminder of the Lord's provision when the Israelites lived in hastily-constructed shelters as they wandered in the wilderness. "Ye shall dwell in booths . . . That your generations may know that I made the children of Israel to dwell in booths, when I brought them out of the land of Egypt: I am the LORD your God" (Leviticus 23:42-43).

The Feast of Tabernacles was designed to keep fresh before succeeding generations how God provided for His people during the forty years of wandering from Egypt to the promised land. Their delays were caused by their own doubts and disobedience. Nevertheless, God brought them to the place He chose for them. He did not want them to forget that He remained faithful in providing all their needs. "Thou shalt remember all the way which the LORD thy God led thee these forty years in the wilderness, to humble thee, and to prove thee, to know what was in thine heart, whether thou wouldest keep His commandments, or no" (Deuteronomy 8:2). It was a fitting climax to the Jewish annual feasts. As the families spent one week each year in those temporary makeshift shelters, they reflected on the faithfulness of God.

Repeatedly in the book of Deuteronomy the people were exhorted to remember. "Only take heed to thyself, and keep thy soul diligently, lest thou forget . . ." (4:9). "Take heed to yourselves, lest ye forget . . . (4:23). "And remember that thou wast a servant in the land of Egypt . . ." (5:15). "Then beware lest thou forget the LORD which brought thee forth out of the land of Egypt, from the house of bondage" (6:12). "Remember what the LORD thy God did unto Pharaoh, and unto all Egypt" (7:18). "Beware that thou forget not the LORD thy God . . ." (8:11). "Then thine heart be lifted up, and thou forget the LORD thy God, which brought thee forth out of the land of Egypt, from the house of bondage" (8:14). "But thou shalt remember the LORD thy God: for it is He that giveth thee power to get wealth . . ." (8:18). "Remember and forget not . . ." (9:7). "And thou shalt remember that thou wast a bondman in the land of Egypt, and the LORD thy God redeemed thee: therefore I command thee this thing today" (15:15). "And thou shalt remember that thou wast a bondman in Egypt: and thou shalt observe and do these statutes" (16:12).

The Feast of Tabernacles was to serve as a reminder to future generations that God was the provider and protector of His people. He had preserved them. In fact, everything they ever had came from Him. One week each year in a crude shelter was to remind them how they once lived. To be deprived of their daily blessings—clothing, food, housing, health, pleasure—just for that one week, would help them to realize how thankful they should be. All those weary desert years were now but memories of their failure and God's faithfulness, when "he fed them according to the integrity of his heart; and guided

115

them by the skilfulness of his hands" (Psalm 78:72). This feast was truly a time to remember. God always delights in His children giving praise and thanksgiving. We must never forget that we are led and fed by the hand of God.

This provides a very practical lesson for our own lives. Our Lord wants His people to retain at all times a spirit of thanksgiving. It is good for us to sit quietly and look back to the sinful past from which God redeemed us. Let us not be too proud to do this. Most of us go to great lengths to hide our humble origins and sinful past. We are deceived into believing that if we hide the true facts about our past, others will think more highly of us, especially if the present is more respectable than the past.

The prophet Isaiah gave some excellent advice when he wrote, "Look unto the rock whence ye are hewn, and to the hole of the pit whence ye are digged" (Isaiah 51:1). May we never forget that our roots reach back to that pit of sin, and admit with the psalmist, "Behold, I was shapen in iniquity; and in sin did my mother conceive me" (Psalm 51:5), and, "He brought me up also out of an horrible pit, out of the miry clay, and set my feet upon a rock, and established by goings" (Psalm 40:2). Let each of us pause to reflect and remember.

A TIME TO REJOICE

This final feast was further a time of rejoicing before the Lord. "Ye shall rejoice before the LORD your God seven days" (Leviticus 23:40). Don't miss the orderly progression here: first the Day of Atonement, then the Feast of Tabernacles. On the Day of Atonement, they expressed affliction of soul (23:27,29,32), a deep sorrow over their sins. Until their sins had been cleansed and forgiven, they could not rejoice. Sin always prevents joy; joy always follows cleansing and forgiveness. When David sinned, he lost his joy. Hear him as he pleads with God: "Restore unto me the joy of thy salvation" (Psalm 51:12). He did not lose his salvation, but he did lose his joy. When we walk in unbroken fellowship with our Lord and keep our confessions up to date, the heart remains joyful. The Feast of Tabernacles was the most joyous of the annual Jewish feasts.

Notice God's words to His people in the following passage:

> "Thou shalt observe the feast of tabernacles seven days, after that thou hast gathered in thy corn and thy wine: And thou shalt rejoice in thy feast, thou, and thy son, and thy daughter, and thy manservant, and thy maidservant, and the Levite, the stranger, and the fatherless, and the widow, that are within thy gates. Seven days shalt thou keep a solemn feast unto the LORD thy God in the place which the LORD shall choose: because the LORD thy God shall bless thee in all thine increase, and in all the works of thine hands, therefore thou shalt surely rejoice" (Deuteronomy 16:13-15).

It was the Lord's intention that this final feast be a time of great rejoicing. "Thou shalt rejoice . . . thou shalt surely rejoice."

How can we account for the extraordinary joy which accompanied the celebration of the Feast of Tabernacles? What precipitated the joyful attitude of the Israelites when the toil and trials of this life were forgotten and their thoughts went back to the past? The answer to these questions is not far removed from us. By a careful review of the first four feasts, in their application to all believers in Christ, a joyous spirit should fill our hearts.

117

Passover. We learned from Scripture that this first feast on God's prophetic calendar had its fulfillment in the death of our Lord Jesus Christ (1 Corinthians 5:7). When the angel Gabriel announced to the virgin Mary the fact of our Lord's incarnation, she said, "My spirit hath rejoiced in God my Saviour" (Luke 1:47). And then at His birth the angel announced, "Behold, I bring you good tidings of great joy, which shall be to all people. For unto you is born this day in the city of David a Saviour, which is Christ the Lord" (Luke 2:10-11).

The first response from the heart of a believing sinner is to rejoice in having heard the gospel and believing it (Acts 13:48; 16:34). If there is one truth more than another which I desire to press to the hearts of God's redeemed children, it is that the Lord Jesus Christ, our Passover, has saved us from the guilt and penalty of our sins. This is a high pinnacle of biblical revelation and of Christian experience, and should cause us to rejoice daily at its very thought. "Rejoice in the Lord alway: and again I say, Rejoice" (Philippians 4:4). Have you paused today to reflect upon our great Savior and His "so great salvation"? (Titus 2:13; Hebrews 2:3). When we remember and reflect daily on our Passover lamb and His wondrous provision for our eternal salvation, our day will be one of joy.

Unleavened Bread. In the "so great salvation" which God has provided for us in Christ, He has also made provision for our sanctification—the practical holiness, the daily confessing and forsaking of "the sin which doth so easily beset us" (Hebrews 12:1). We know from the teaching of Scripture, as well as from our own personal experience, that holiness of life is the harbinger of joy. Where holiness enters, a glow of joy is expressed.

When we consider the pictures of our Lord given to us by Matthew, Mark, Luke, and John, we see in Him "the beauty

118

of holiness." In His matchless manhood there was a holiness unequaled by any other. His friends and followers who knew Him best, as well as those enemies who hated Him most, never once found a flaw in His moral character. In our dear Passover lamb holiness is displayed uniquely. His holiness has no parallel in the human race.

In God's prophetic calendar, Passover marked a new beginning for every sinner who would trust Christ for salvation. "Therefore if any man be in Christ, he is a new creature: old things are passed away; behold, all things are become new" (2 Corinthians 5:17). A born-again person is the product of the creative act of the holy God, what he has become in Christ "the Holy One of God" (Luke 4:34). But the work of salvation included more, much more. When we received Christ we became "partakers of the divine nature" (2 Peter 1:4) and therefore "partakers of his holiness" (Hebrews 12:10). In the Greek that word *partaker (koinōnos)* means having in common, sharing jointly in a common partnership.

The New Testament Epistles make much of this imparted holiness. The Holy Spirit who indwells us is called "the Spirit of holiness" (Romans 1:4). God chose us in Christ "that we should be holy" (Ephesians 1:4), and then He exhorts us to "put on the new man, which after God is created in righteousness and true holiness" (4:24). "Even so now yield your members servants to righteousness unto holiness" and "have your fruit unto holiness" (Romans 6:19-22). "For God hath not called us unto uncleanness, but unto holiness" (1 Thessalonians 4:7).

Sin is a destroyer of joy. Our sins hurt the Lord Jesus more than we can ever know. In the classic passage from the pen of the prophet Isaiah our Redeemer is depicted as "a man of sorrows, and acquainted with grief" (53:3). The reason for this

119

description of Him is obvious. "He was wounded for our trans-gressions, he was bruised for our iniquities" (53:5). As He moved closer to Calvary, Matthew wrote that He "began to be sorrowful and very heavy" (26:37). Mark records His very words. "My soul is exceeding sorrowful unto death" (14:34). Yes, our sins brought sorrow to the holy Son of God. And our sins will bring sorrow to our own hearts. A little sin in the life of a Christian will steal the joy from the heart. Holiness both experiences and expresses joy.

Firstfruits. We see two very important lessons to be applied to every believer in Christ as we examine the Feast of Firstfruits. The first is *stewardship,* a present responsibility enjoined upon every child of God. When we become genuinely and experien-tially saved and open wide our hearts to the sanctifying power of God's Word, something happens which causes us to see everything in a new way. We learn that our dear Savior is the creator and controller of the earth and all its contents (Psalm 24:1; Haggai 2:8). We learn further that we must honor Him with our substance (Proverbs 3:9) and seek first His kingdom and His righteousness (Matthew 6:33). Then there comes unto us a new controlling force producing a new spiritual joy. The Christians at Corinth learned well this truth. Paul wrote of them, "How that in a great trial of afflication the abundance of their joy and their deep poverty abounded unto the riches of their liberality" (2 Corinthians 8:2). No unregenerate mind can pos-sibly breach the gulf between those two statements: "the abun-dance of their joy . . . and their deep poverty." Here is a great paradox. Yet it is blessedly true, as Paul reminded the elder at Ephesus, "Remember the words of the Lord Jesus, how he said, It is more blessed to give than to receive" (Acts 20:35). "It is required in stewards, that a man be found faithful" (1 Corinthians 4:2). So if we would know the continual joy of the

120

Lord—that exulting, exuberant joy—we must be faithful stewards.

Another lesson seen in the Feast of Firstfruits is the fact of the Christian's future *security*. God's prophetic calendar commenced with the Passover, the type having its fulfillment in the death of our Lord Jesus Christ who was sacrificed for us (1 Corinthians 5:7). And in that same Epistle to the Corinthians, the apostle unfolds the next event in God's calendar. We know that our Lord's resurrection from death and the tomb followed His death and burial. Christ arose from the dead, and so all who believed in Christ will be raised; "Christ the Firstfruits, afterward they that are Christ's at his coming!" (1 Corinthians 15:23).

An interesting fact in connection with the seven convocations is the time they were first given. God revealed them to Moses while the Hebrews were wandering in the desert. There was a great future ahead for Israel, promised by God while His people were struggling. Many of them suffered and died during the wilderness journey. There is still a future for Israel which has not yet been harvested. That nation's greatest joy will be their portion when Messiah returns and the people recognize and receive Him.

There is a lesson here for us Christians. When we were born again we received new life, the very life of Christ Himself (Galatians 2:20). When He arose, we were raised in Him. When He ascended, we ascended in Him (Ephesians 2:4-6). But there is a part of us that must wait for the final harvest; so we are waiting for the redemption of our bodies (Romans 8:23). Christians have suffered in the past. Many of God's children are suffering now. And so it will be until Christ returns and the final harvest is complete. Then we shall be like Him, made absolutely perfect in spirit and in our bodies. Christ is our firstfruits. At His coming every part of us will be harvested, even those parts which give us pain and problems now. "Being confident of this very thing, that he which hath begun a good work in you will perform it until the day of Jesus Christ" (Philippians 1:6).

Brothers and sisters in Christ, the greatest joy is yet to come. The sanctifying of Christ the firstfruits guarantees the entire harvest: "For if the firstfruit be holy, the lump is also holy" (Romans 11:16). Tabernacles is the seventh feast, lasting seven days in the seventh month, a trilogy of sevens. God is telling us here of a complete and perfect salvation with its complete and perfect joy when our Lord returns. Salvation does have a definite fulfillment, a perfect consummation, a time of great rejoicing. The best is yet to come.

Pentecost. The waiting period between Christ's first coming and His final coming was not without divine provision for His disciples. When He told them of His intention of leaving them and returning to His Father in heaven, they were deeply saddened. Their hearts were "troubled" (John 14:1). Joy had gone from them. At the news of His leaving them they felt like orphans, so He said "I will not leave you comfortless" (John 14:18), meaning, "as orphans." He said further, "Ye shall be sorrowful, but your sorrow shall be turned into joy" (John 16:20). What would cause their sorrow to be turned into joy? The answer is unmistakably clear. The coming of the Holy Spirit at Pentecost would provide the needed joy. And that is precisely what happened. "The disciples were filled with joy, and with the Holy Ghost" (Acts 13:2).

Let us not fail to grasp the lesson to be applied in the life and experience of every one of us. Looking more closely at Acts 13:2, take special note of that twofold filling, "filled with joy, and with the Holy Ghost." The Spirit-filled Christian is a joyful person because "the fruit of the Spirit is . . . joy" (Galatians 5:22). Yes, on the day of Pentecost the Spirit came. He has taken up a permanent residence in every saved person. When He controls us, sadness is replaced with joy.

But the Feast of Tabernacles, along with the two feasts preceding it, Trumpets and Atonement, all await a future fulfillment with special emphasis on the nation Israel. This last feast on God's prophetic calendar points to the earthly reign of Israel's Messiah, our Lord Jesus Christ.

Christ's Coming Kingdom

IN MY INTRODUCTORY REMARKS to this study in Leviticus 23, I pointed out that the seven feasts were arranged by God chronologically to present His own prophetic program. The time period in God's calendar commenced with Passover, with its fulfillment in the death of Christ. In that divinely-planned event, consummated on the cross at Calvary, a clear picture was given to us of *God's plan of salvation.*

The Feast of Unleavened Bread came next. The student is not left in doubt as to the meaning of this second feast. The Bible is a self-interpretive book, consisting of two major parts: the Old and New Testaments. The New is in the Old concealed; the Old is in the New revealed. Thus we learned from the New Testament that the Feast of Unleavened Bread presented *God's provision for sanctification.*

The Feast of Firstfruits was the next event in God's prophetic calendar, predicting the bodily resurrection of our Lord from death and the grave. According to God's calendar He did rise on the third day after His death. The meaning for the Christian was made clear by the apostle Paul in 1 Corinthians 15:23. The resurrection of Christ gives assurance that those believers in Christ who have died will be raised. For the Christian, that Feast of Firstfruits is *God's pledge of security.*

The first three feasts had their fulfillment with the first coming of Christ to the earth. As we look back on God's calendar, they are now history. The fourth feast, Pentecost, is where we presently are on God's calendar. The Holy Spirit came on the day of Pentecost. We are living in the dispensation which began on that very day. The last three feasts—Trumpets, Atonement, and Tabernacles—all await a future fulfillment. The Feast of Tabernacles, the last of the seven holy convocations in God's prophetic calendar, has a prophetic aspect. That great future when God's purpose will be accomplished is the major theme in this final study.

In the chapter preceding this present one, we saw how the Feast of Tabernacles was a time for *remembering* and *rejoicing*. But in its larger fulfillment it is preeminently a time set apart and appointed by God for the manifestation of His power and glory. The Scriptures depict that future as a time of restitution.

The fulfillment of the great Feast of Tabernacles is prophetic of the final coming of Christ to earth when He sets up His millennial kingdom. It speaks of the full and final restoration of all things. The time of Christ's coming kingdom was in the thoughts of both His friends and His foes. The Pharisees pressed Him to tell them "when the kingdom of God should come" (Luke 17:20). The final question from our Lord's own followers immediately before His ascension was, "Lord, wilt thou at this time restore again the kingdom to Israel?" (Acts 1:6). The age of peace and blessing on earth has been man's hope since the fall of Adam in Eden.

Peter spoke of that bright future not long after Pentecost when he said, "And [God] shall send Jesus Christ, which before was preached unto you: Whom the heavens must receive until the times of restitution of all things, which God hath spoken by the mouth of all his holy prophets since the world began"

(Acts 3:20-21). Yes, God has a fixed time on His calendar for the "restitution of all things" and the restoration and rest of both Israel and the Gentiles. This is in keeping with the character of Old Testament prophets and their prophecies. They wrote of the future time when Messiah's work would be accomplished and His kingdom established fully and finally.

The Feast of Tabernacles cannot be disassociated from the earthly reign of Israel's Messiah, the Lord Jesus Christ. The prophet Zechariah linked together these two events. Before we examine a small portion of Zechariah's prophecy, I would caution the student of the Bible to guard against spiritualizing those events of which the prophet speaks, merely because no fulfillment has yet been found in history. There is a future messianic kingdom, a literal reign of righteousness and peace on earth. Palestine will be its geographical center with Israel as the prominent and prevailing nation. Jerusalem with its temple will be rebuilt, Israel will be restored, and the whole earth will experience a glorious restitution. Zechariah wrote of this sure and solemn prophecy which is yet to be literally fulfilled, and he clearly associated it with the Feast of Tabernacles.

> And his feet shall stand in that day upon the mount of Olives which is before Jerusalem (Zechariah 14:4). And the LORD shall be king over all the earth: in that day shall there be one LORD, and his name one (14:9). And it shall come to pass, that every one that is left of all the nations which came against Jerusalem shall even go up from year to year to worship the king the LORD of hosts, and to keep the feast of tabernacles. And it shall be, that whoso will not come up of all the families of the earth unto Jerusalem to worship the king, the LORD of hosts, even upon them shall be no rain. And if the family of Egypt go not up,

and come not, that have no rain, there shall be the plague, wherewith the LORD will smite the heathen that come not up to keep the feast of tabernacles. This shall be the punishment of Egypt, and the punishment of all nations that come not up to keep the feast of tabernacles (14,16-19).

Conservative scholars are in agreement that the one whose feet shall stand upon the Mount of Olives (14:4), and who shall be Lord and King over all the earth (14:9) is none other than the Son of God, the Lord Jesus Christ. When He comes, He will appear from the very place that was His mountain, called the Mount of Olives. It was from this mountain that He delivered His great prophetic discourse (Matthew 24–25) and to which He returned with His disciples after He kept the Passover and instituted His supper (Matthew 26:30). Finally, He led His disciples to Bethany (on the Mount of Olives) "and he lifted up his hands, and blessed them, And it came to pass, while he blessed them, he was parted from them, and carried up into heaven" (Luke 24:50-51). It is on that holy mount where He will appear, the same mount from which He ascended to heaven. Zechariah prophesied the exact location of Christ's return to earth.

Zechariah associates the King and His kingdom with the Feast of Tabernacles. But why is this one feast singled out to be observed in Christ's coming kingdom? Commentators differ in their answers to this question. Briefly, I will offer a suggestion or two. First, nothing in the last two thousand years, since the death of Christ, has come even close to resembling the Feast of Tabernacles. We have seen the orderly and progressive arrangement of the first six feasts in God's prophetic calendar; therefore, I have concluded that the fulfillment of the seventh feast is yet in the future.

Second, the prophet foretold that the feast will be held when the King is reigning in Jerusalem (14:8-9). The third part of Isaiah's compound prophecy has never been fulfilled, namely, "The government shall be upon his shoulder" (Isaiah 9:6). The mystery of this Old Testament prophecy can be solved only by comparing it with the many additional prophecies in Scripture which deal with Christ's reign of peace on earth. According to God's calendar, this great coming event will unfold itself in the course of time.

Notice further that the nations will come to Jerusalem every year to worship the King, the Lord Jesus Christ, and to keep the Feast of Tabernacles (Zechariah 14:16). Those who refuse to come to the feast to worship Him will be judged by Him (14:17). In our present dispensation, God does not compel anyone to worship Him. Someone has estimated that of all the people on earth, only approximately one-sixth of the total population worship God. Many of those who refuse to receive the Lord Jesus Christ have in their control great material prosperity. God is not now judging them. On the contrary, "He maketh his sun to rise on the evil and on the good, and sendeth rain on the just and on the unjust" (Matthew 5:45). But the time is coming when those who refuse to worship the King will get no rain. God has written in His calendar a time when, at the mention of the name of Jesus, every knee shall bow and "every tongue should confess that Jesus Christ is Lord, to the glory of God the Father" (Philippians 2:9-11).

Did you ever wonder why no one is requested, or required, to keep the Feast of Passover or Firstfruits or Pentecost? These all have to do with the present church age, all of which will be past history in that future day. The Feast of Tabernacles has to do with Christ's coming kingdom on earth. It is the last of the seven feasts, the final event in God's prophetic calendar.

Following the restoration of the remnant of Israel and the restitution of all things, including nature itself, the unsaved people of the Gentile nations who turn to God and receive His Son will enter into the kingdom and enjoy the peace and rest that Christ alone can give.

Look again at Peter's post-pentecostal message: "And [God] shall send Jesus Christ, which before was preached unto you: Whom the heavens must receive until the times of restitution of all things, which God hath spoken by the mouth of all his holy prophets since the world began" (Acts 3:20-21). God's prophets lived and died. They were mere men, and are gone, but their divinely-inspired and eternal words remain with us. Here is but one statement from the pen of the prophet Isaiah: "And the ransomed of the LORD shall return, and come to Zion with songs and everlasting joy upon their heads: they shall obtain joy and gladness, and sorrow and sighing shall flee away" (Isaiah 35:10). This is but one of the hundreds of passages written by God's prophets which tells of the consummation of man's rebellion against God and the commencement of Christ's glorious reign. Then one could add to the Old Testament prophets the mighty prediction of the apostle John, who wrote, "And I heard a great voice out of heaven saying, Behold, the tabernacle of God is with men, and he will dwell with them, and they shall be his people, and God himself shall be with them, and be their God" (Revelation 21:3).

The major theme in the book of Leviticus is *holiness,* the word "holy" appearing not less than ninety-one times. Frequently God said to His people, "Ye shall be holy; for I am holy" (11:44-45; 19:2; 20:7,26; 21:8).

When the last of seven solemn assemblies is fulfilled, the Feast of Tabernacles, holiness will shine forth at last. Take special note of those closing words of Zechariah's prophecy:

In that day shall there be upon the bells of the horses, Holiness unto the LORD; and the pots in the LORD's house shall be like the bowls before the altar. Yea, every pot in Jerusalem and in Judah shall be holiness unto the LORD of hosts: and all they that sacrifice shall come and take of them, and seethe therein: and in that day there shall be no more the Canaanite in the house of the LORD of hosts (Zeechariah 14:20-21).

Holiness unto the Lord will be the prominent slogan during the kingdom age. When the final feast on God's calendar comes to pass "holiness" will be a popular topic of conversation. It will be written on people and on their possessions, including household goods and cooking utensils as well as pots and pans.

During my fifty years in the ministry I have been an invited guest in literally hundreds of Christian homes. In many of them I saw plaques, hanging on the wall or placed on a piece of furniture, containing a verse from the Bible, or a well-known piece of prose or poetry. The following is one I have seen many times:

Christ is the head of this house, The unseen guest at every meal, The silent listener to every conversation.

In some homes where these words appear the people who live there put them into practice. This is not always the case. But in Christ's kingdom, both private and domestic life will be holy. Everything shall be holy in that day.

The greatest fact of the *past* is that the Lord Jesus Christ appeared on this earth for a period of thirty-three years. In the wisdom and plan of God the Father, planet earth is precisely where He should have been at that time, for then " he appeared to put away sin by the sacrifice of himself" (Hebrews 9:26).

The greatest fact of the *present* is that the same Lord Jesus Christ appears in heaven, highly exalted by God the Father. In the wisdom and plan of God, heaven is precisely where He should be now. He entered "into heaven itself, now to appear in the presence of God for us" (Hebrews 9:24).

The greatest fact of the *future* is that this same Lord Jesus Christ will return to earth. When He comes, in the wisdom and plan of God, the earth is precisely where He should be. "And unto them that look for him shall he appear the second time without sin unto salvation" (Hebrews 9:28).

The King is coming! "And the seventh angel sounded; and there were great voices in heaven, saying, The kingdoms of this world are become the kingdoms of our Lord, and of his Christ; and he shall reign for ever and ever" (Revelation 11:15). What a kingdom! What a King! How blessed will be that day when believing Israel and believing Gentiles bow before God's beloved Son!

> Unto him that loved us, and washed us from our sins in his own blood. And hath made us kings and priests unto God and his Father; to him be glory and dominion for ever and ever. Amen (Revelation 1:5-6).

Bibliography

Baron, David. 1972. *The Visions and Prophecies of Zechariah*. Grand Rapids, Michigan.

Bucksbazen, Victor. 1954. *The Gospel in the Feasts of Israel*. Philadelphia.

Erdman, Charles R. 1951. *The Book of Leviticus*. Ada, Michigan: Baker Book House Co.

Goldberg, Louis. 1980. *Leviticus*. Grand Rapids, Michigan: Zondervan Publishing House.

Gustafson, Roy W. 1958. *Feasting on the Feasts*. Findlay, Ohio.

Heslop, W. G. 1945. *Lessons from Leviticus*. Grand Rapids, Michigan: Kregel Publications.

Holiday, A. J. *The Feasts of the Lord*. London.

Kellogg, S. H. 1916. *The Book of Leviticus*. London.

Mackintosh, C. H. 1881. *Notes on the Pentateuch*. Neptune, New Jersey: Loizeaux Brothers, Inc.

McGee, J. Vernon. 1975. *Leviticus*. Pasadena, California.

Newell, William. 1950. *Studies in the Pentateuch*. Grand Rapids, Michigan: Kregel Publications.

Nichols, J. W. H. 1938. *The Feasts of the Lord*. New York.

Ritchie, John. 1895. *The Feasts of Jehovah*. Grand Rapids, Michigan: Kregel Publications.

Thompson, Robert. 1975. *The Feasts of the Lord*. Medford, Oregon: Omega Pubns.

Van Ryn, August. 1944. *His Appointments*. New York.

Wiersbe, Warren W. 1982. *Be God's Guest*. Lincoln, Nebraska: Back to the Bible.

Willis, G. C. 1957. *The Seven Feasts of Jehovah*. Hong Kong.